VIEW

from the

LAUNDRY CHUTE

VIEW from the LAUNDRY CHUTE

D. Klein

CHAPTER TWO PRESS ◊ SAFETY HARBOR, FL

VIEW FROM THE LAUNDRY CHUTE
Copyright © 2019 by Deborah Klein.
All rights reserved. Published by Chapter Two Press.

No part of this book may be used or reproduced in any manner whatsoever without written permission except in the case of brief quotations embodied in critical articles or reviews. For more information, address Chapter Two Press, P. O. Box 870, Safety Harbor, FL 34695.

www.chaptertwopress.com

This is a work of semi-fiction. The characters, places and events in this book are partially the product of the author's imagination, meaning fabrication combined with fragments of reality. With the limited exception of friends and relatives who are periodically mentioned (you know who you are), any similarity to real persons, living or dead, is coincidental, and *not*, (sorta) intended by the author.

Library of Congress Control Number: 2020906708

First Edition: December 2020
10 9 8 7 6 5 4 3 2 1

Printed in the United States of America.
Book design by Warren Firschein
The text type was set in Adobe Jenson.

Dedicated to Kristin

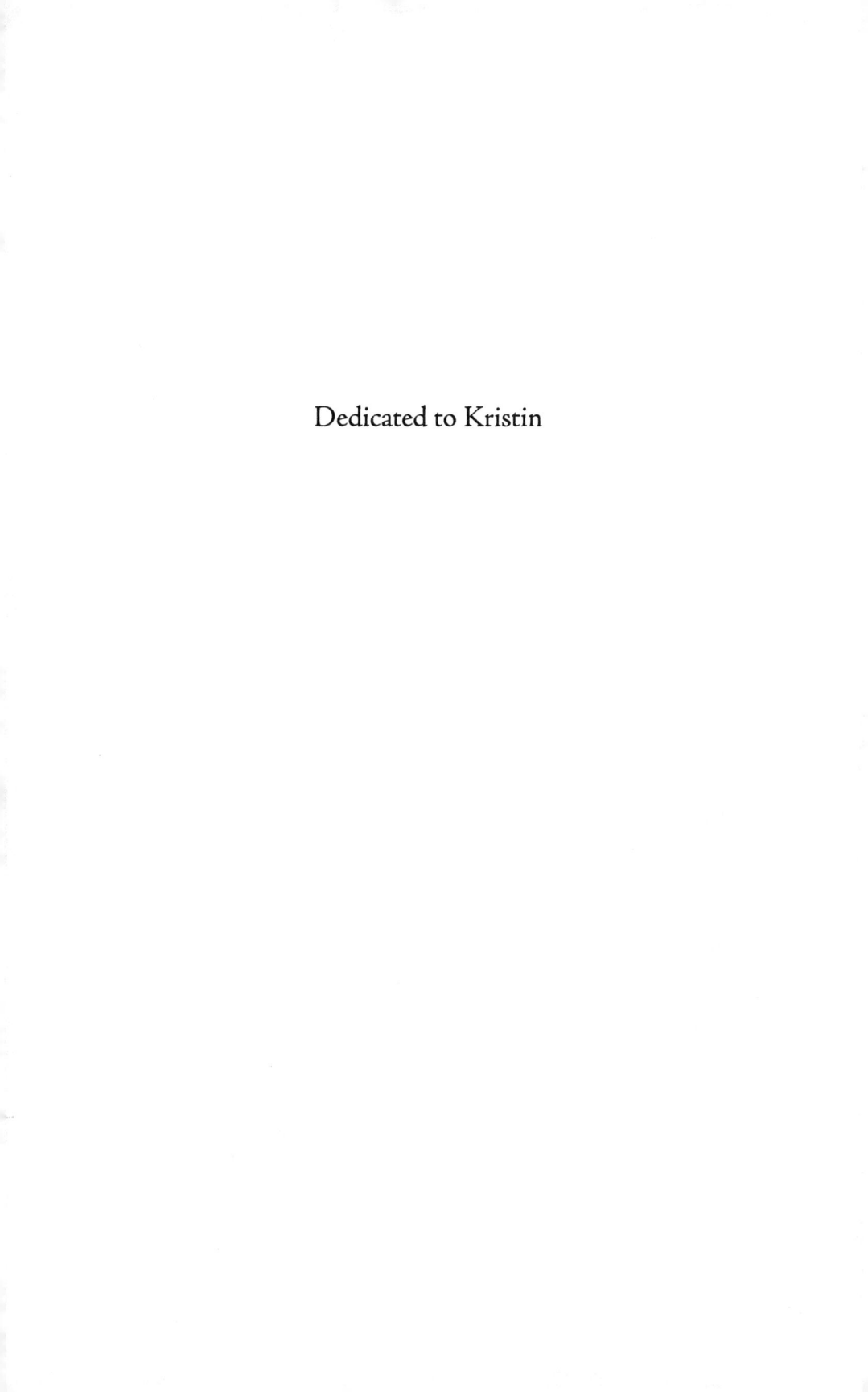

TABLE OF CONTENTS

Introduction i
Being Debbie 1
To a Degree 3
Hope For $49.95 8
The Wake 12
The Hop-To-It Diet 16
The Laundry Chute 24
At Your Own Risk 27
Under the Table 30
Autumn of 1967 32
Stilettos and Mt. McKinley 38
Dear God 44
This Is Your Brain At Funerals 48
Getting Picky About Aging 54
I Am Curious (Cheeseburger) 59
Handle With Care 64
L.W.P. 70
On Being Fat 74
The Theater 77
Bicycles 81
Another Thought 82

Pica Di Uh-Oh 84
Lingo in Cubesville 88
Mailing Ernie 93
Fear of Flinging 98
Repetition Repeats Itself. 103
Hold the Tomatoes. 108
Quantum Physics and Thai Food. 110
The Cookout 115
It's the Journey. 121
Acknowledgements. 125
About the Author. 129

INTRODUCTION

I was sanctified by frogs on a gritty, brown beach at Geneva-on-the-Lake in the summer of 1954. I sprouted legs and crawled into the corner of the coffee table, earning six stitches. I also crawled into a laundry chute thinking I'd find Alice and the Mad Hatter. I morphed to walking, then climbing, then hopping from job to job and man to man, not realizing the frogs that blanketed my parents after their coupling would translate to my course in life, or, as my sister suspects, that my mother's bad temperament while she carried me would contribute to my depressive nature. These are the mystical happenings in life, which *might* explain a variety of jobs, migrations back and forth to Florida, a fondness for rainy days, a love of frogs, my fertile imagination, and a long list of medications.

I spent most of my childhood sitting in a tree or on top of a doghouse in our back yard. To say I was introspective would be an understatement. That would be like saying you should consider that holding a metal rod up in a violent thunderstorm might be a bad idea.

VIEW FROM THE LAUNDRY CHUTE

My menses at the age of nine, mixed with this introspection, careened me into a sad and humiliating adolescence.

High school brought with it a first love and all the tingly, feverish feelings that go with that particular rite of passage. Soon after, I discovered drugs and sex.

I went from high school to college where I lasted exactly a month. I quit one of the best schools in the state. Ohio University was fondly known as "Harvard on the Hocking." Dad reminded me—often—that if I had quit one week earlier he'd have been refunded in full for the semester. Timing is everything. I moved back home, then hopped down to Florida, back home, down to Florida, back home, and down to Florida, where I will probably stay until they put my ashes in a shoebox.

I get excited about frogs and toads. I talk to them frequently. I scold them for hanging out in the street. I even stop the car to gather them up and relocate them. It can take an eternity for me to get somewhere after it rains. There are a lot of misguided hoppers out there. I've even kissed a few, but it never got me anywhere.

It's been a wild ride for sure, from a fall down a tin-lined laundry chute to the day my AARP card arrived in the mail. These stories are like little tchotchkes found at the bottom of a cluttered closet that I rummage through on dark and stormy nights. I like to pull them out and examine them from time to time.

BEING DEBBIE

I used to be hot. I was. But I never thought so, even then. So it was a totally wasted hot.

In fact, *I Used to be Hot* was originally going to be the title of this book until I realized that there are only a couple of stories that describe my deterioration. And stories about getting old have become pretty uncool. Uncool and boring. So that *almost*-title would belabor a subject I'd rather mention less.

Writing has been a passion since I created stories while sitting on top of our beagle's doghouse in the back yard as a small child. It didn't matter if it was summer or winter. There I would sit, like a jockey on a horse, knees pulled up, and thighs gripping the pitch of the roof. I wrote down the stories I imagined in an old notebook. Then I would try to sell them door-to-door for a quarter each, in my Ohio neighborhood.

Going back to touch briefly on my deterioration, the last several years have been tough, so I've not aged gracefully. I often picture myself in a nursing home. The CNAs will flip a coin to see who has to bathe me.

"She threw poop at me yesterday. I hate that old bitch."

I perform at Open Mics and various events sometimes. I have a poem called "Better in a Burka" that I read with a bag over my head. The basic gist of the poem—burkas as cover-ups for all the stuff I've bitched about concerning my body. But I expanded the poem to include many kinds of people, like those who have had bad plastic surgery. After putting that bag over my head a few times, it dawned on me that I am actually pretty authentic. I've earned every wrinkle, every roll, every gnarl. At least I don't look like someone whose ponytail is pulled too tight. Still, the poem is funnier with the bag.

Also, it occurred to me that constantly whining about not being hot anymore was, in itself, a kind of sick vanity. So, for the last few years I have declared *fuck it*. I don't care that I'm thick in the middle and I have no neck. So what about the veins on my legs! And my breasts? Well, never mind. The point is, I am *better*. I'm far more creative now than I've ever been! I may have *looked* better years ago, but I didn't *think* better. My wit is sharper. My writing has improved. Shit, the possibilities are endless!

Bring on the cameras! I will no longer dive behind people or statues or grassy knolls. I don't have a "best side" because *all* my sides, especially the *inside*, are good sides. Good enough for me anyway.

TO A DEGREE

Every year, at colleges all across the country, the hats will be flung into the air. Parents will remember their children as the little boys and girls that they used to be. The graduates will be anxious to go home to cold showers and envelopes on kitchen counters from well-wishers. Will there be enough in them to rent an apartment? Parents will wonder the same thing.

We'll have a new crop of degreed Target sales people, veterinary assistants, baristas at Starbucks, dog walkers, servers, and Mary Kay representatives who are nannies on the side.

I contend that this new degreed herd will not necessarily be smarter—just more in debt. I know this because I've worked with them over the years. There's a good chance they can't even spell. But who am I to judge? I flunked out of college my first quarter.

No ... WAIT, dammit, I'll *tell* you who I am to judge.

I am a semi-old woman with so much experience in just about everything that my head might explode if I learn one more fucking thing. I've pounded the bottoms into foot-stools with a rubber mallet in a factory where big-haired women sat at sewing machines and sang along to Tammy Wynette on the radio.

I've pumped gas and checked oil during the gas shortage of the seventies—in blizzards. The disgusting owner thought it would be a good idea to have pretty girls as gas attendants. But we had to wear ski masks and snowsuits or we'd freeze to death. He yelled at us and told us we looked like "little monkeys." We quit before the weather broke. God only knows what he would have had us wear in the summer.

I mixed drinks for bookies and the mafia at the Solar Lounge in Youngstown. It was below a motel. The bookies worked in a room upstairs. I knew the difference between the girlfriends and the wives. I started at nine a.m. My first customer was always the motel manager. He'd come in for a shot of J&B and a beer, his gut distended and tight, straining against his yellowed undershirt. He'd leer at me while I scraped burnt hot dogs off a rotating spit because the damned thing was left on all night, the rancid smell of beer and grease wafting up from the machine.

I managed a blue jeans store. The owners once even flew me to Chicago to view a new line. They were impressed when I came back with sketches. I often chased shoplifters out of the store and stood in front of their cars, pounding the hoods, screaming threats and obscenities at the thieves whose eyes peered over steering wheels.

Then, when the franchise went under, I hypocritically helped myself to three pairs of jeans.

I'm always honest on applications. Q. Have you ever stolen anything? A. Yes.

(If ANYONE answers that question any other way, they are lying.)

I arranged flowers for a florist for one week until the owner stood over me one too many times while I tried to take Florafax orders over the phone. She corrected everything I said so that I couldn't understand the person on the other end. I swung around in my seat with the boldness of youth and yelled, "I DO have a BRAIN, you bitch!"

I pressure-cleaned cars for dealerships. We'd meet at the cleaning company and pile into the back of a pick-up at five a.m. where we'd huddle against the equipment and drink coffee. We wore cut-offs, t-shirts, and doo-rags. I was easily ten years older than the rest, but could still sing along to Led Zeppelin with them. I hated Led Zeppelin. We'd barrel across the bridge to Tampa and I'd pray that no one from my previous job would see me. I'd gone from a salaried job in Tampa to five bucks an hour cleaning cars. But it was better than selling custom-made thong bikinis, which I also did for five bucks an hour until they let me go for being overqualified. I rearranged the whole store my second day. (I really liked that job.)

I was a bookkeeper in a nursing home, audited hospitals for the Federal Government, processed claims for Aetna, became a massage therapist, worked in a print-shop and knew how to operate an electric jack while keeping twenty-two pockets of a Kolbus binder from running out of paper. I wrapped everything from shirts to five-foot plastic palm trees at a wrap desk in a department store during the Christmas season . . . for crazy people. I mixed amalgam for a dentist and held people's lips aside while he drilled and also ran out to buy his booze during breaks. I worked for commission at a cosmetics counter. I sold cement, not that different from cosmetics. I knew what chat mix was and how many pounds per square inch it would take to pour a patio. I waitressed between these jobs plus raised a child, pretty much alone.

But I don't have a degree, because you can't LEARN the amount of things I know in any class taught by anybody in either four or four *hundred* years.

I watched recently as Ben Affleck and Oprah Winfrey were awarded honorary degrees by Brown and Harvard Universities, respectively. SO, it is in this spirit of getting a degree without having to attend classes and accrue a lifetime of debt that I have decided to award myself an honorary Master's Degree.

It is a Master's Degree for being a Skilled Human of Immeasurable Talents.

And, as a person with a SHIT degree, there is no job too daunting and no bank account too depleted for me to deal with. Plus, I'm as faithful as an old beagle when it comes to showing up for work every day. I don't flirt with men in the office because I've totally forgotten how, and, realistically, they wouldn't be receptive anyway.

Let the young brainiacs, fresh from the hallowed halls, twist in the wind a bit, at least until us old high school graduates can make enough money for a decent funeral.

How do they know which hat is theirs, anyway, after they all hit the ground?

HOPE FOR $49.95

Dr. Zot is making me poor and fat.

I believe I've tried all of Zot's (not his real name because I can't afford a lawsuit) "sure-things." I deserve to be on a first name basis with him since I probably paid for the front bumper of his Ferrari. The network I listen to in the morning plays teasers for his afternoon show, "Dr. Zot's Miracle Cures." I can hear it while I examine my stomach before a shower.

"Catch Dr. Zot today at four to hear about the three foods that will guarantee you to lose *nine pounds* a week!"

The first time I paid attention was when he mentioned saffron. As soon as I got home from work I Googled Zot/Saffron. There he was with the miracle pill, a specially formulated extract of saffron. All you had to do was take one before each meal with LOTS of water. I ordered it. It was $49.95 a bottle. I was beside myself with anticipation so I ate a small bag of chips to calm down.

When the box arrived, I ripped it open and swallowed TWO pills to get a head-start. I checked the mirror to see if it was working and laughed at my silliness. *Of course it's not working, it will take at least a few days!*

By the end of the week I had bloated like a toad and couldn't stop belching. I think my skin had turned a pale yellow, but it's hard to tell because that's kinda my natural shade anyway. Plus, there was a Donovan song brain worm in my head every time I took one of the damned things. Saffron was definitely not mad about me.

After two weeks of waddling around like a pregnant woman, I was anything but a mellow yellow. I was pissed. I vowed that I'd NEVER buy his damned miracle pills again.

It was too late. I was already a Zot demographic. Every time I logged on, the pop-up ads for the NEXT Dr. Zot diet, currently making a hit in Hollywood, ambushed me on the screen. I'd hear the same ads on TV that reinforced the pop-ups. Once, he told the audience about a supplement that could literally EXPLODE the fat cells in the body. Everyone would lose weight, *guaranteed*.

My miracle man asked a tearful woman if she was ready to change her life.

There, behind her, was a huge photo of the poor thing in her underwear and sports bra. I cringed. He demonstrated how blueberry ketonics literally *disintegrate* fat. He used balloons filled with water that were frozen and lined up in a box, then he poured some kind of stuff over them that made them burst and melt away. I had to admit it was a cool demonstration. It was certainly better than the time he had actual human fat, freshly suctioned from someone's belly, in a big glass jar.

I called and ordered a box of blueberry ketonic supplements for $49.95. A representative called back to tell me that if I threw in another ten bucks she'd send me TWO boxes. I visualized my fat exploding as my stomach shrank away to nothing. I agreed and threw in another ten, then I ate a small bag of chips to celebrate.

When the box with two bottles of the stuff arrived I ripped it open and took three of them to kick-start the week. I pictured them coursing their way down my esophagus in a rush of water to land in pillows of yellow fat. I could SEE, in my mind, the fat exploding and melting away.

In two days, I was again bloated like a toad and couldn't move without farting. Those fat cells *exploded* all right. But I was determined to finish both bottles.

I gained six pounds. I cursed Dr. Zot whenever I heard the morning ads for his show. I'd rush from the bathroom and flip him the bird with both hands.

A few months later my stomach reminded me of a medicine ball. I could actually lift it up and drop it as if it were a separate entity. I looked at a picture of myself at forty. In it I'm smiling with my daughter in Atlanta. I weighed 127 pounds. I had just had my belly-button pierced in Little Five Points.

Now I could no longer see my naval ring because my stomach ate it.

As I was writing one evening, another pop-up ad caught my attention. Dr. Zot had a supplement that was touted all over the world, not *just* Hollywood. Not only did it make you lose pounds, but it extended your life! This formula was the purest and best.

"You bastard!" I yelled as I sat on hold to place my order. I received my green coffee bean extract for $49.95 a couple days later. I ate some chips and ripped open the box. The minimum balance due on my Visa card had doubled.

I've been taking them faithfully for two weeks now. My stomach is a balloon. I think if you attached a basket to my feet I might be able to carry people through the sky over open farmland. But I *will* take them all. The fact that I will means that I'm a *hopeful* person ... or unbelievably gullible.

I still rush to the TV every morning and whip the bird at his smiling, skinny face. He's smiling because I've now paid for the *back* bumper of his Ferrari.

THE WAKE

My very first hamster was a baby Syrian gold. My Aunt Vera bought him for me on one of our all-day Saturday shopping excursions. I'm not sure Mom was onboard with the adoption after dealing with the dismay of finding a salamander on her Hoover, and pill bugs in my pockets.

Tinkerbell was a fine hamster. I'm reasonably sure he didn't actually COME from Syria, any more than Siamese cats come from Siam. Plus, there isn't a Siam anymore. Perhaps Siamese should be called Thaiese. Anyway, Syrian golden hamsters are the most common kind. They are a reddish-brown and usually have white bellies.

I thought Tinkerbell was a girl. It turns out that little male hamsters have impressive scrotums when they grow up. Not that hamsters get terribly big as adults. I'd estimate that a fat hamster probably does not weigh more than three or four ounces (with empty pouches).

I loved that little guy and carried him around in my shirt pocket. I liked to blow raspberries on his pudgy white tummy. If he became too frisky, I could pick him up by the skin on the back of his neck, like cats do with kittens. He would hang from my fingers like a little man whose parachute got caught in a tree. The sound of his squeaking wheel lulled me to sleep at night. He'd run all night.

Tinkerbell was game for challenges. I'd hand him sunflower seeds one at a time and watch him shove them into his pouches that extended from his jaws to his shoulders. He'd fill those things so full you could barely see his face, only a pink nose which gave him a kind of "ass face." He'd look as if he might explode. The best part was watching him push the seeds out into a pile in the corner of his pen where he kept his stash.

He did a little running in the day if I was home from school (I'd wake him up). He had a special Lucite ball with air holes and a convex lid that screwed on. Tink had his run of the house in that thing. We always knew approximately where he was because the ball made a "pock" sound when he ran into things. If the pocking stopped, it meant either he was taking a nap, a bath, or the lid had come off. I dreaded when the lid came off. We had a cat.

One weekend my cousin Janie came over and we were playing in my room. I went to the kitchen to see if there were any snacks. When I came back, I slid onto the bed like I was sliding in to home base. My arm landed on Tinkerbell. Janie had taken him out to play. He began to gasp. Dad was home so I rushed to the living room

VIEW FROM THE LAUNDRY CHUTE

choking on hot tears while trying to tell him that Tinker was hurt . . . that I hurt him and now he was going to die!

Dad laid him on the kitchen counter and attempted mouth-to-mouth resuscitation and one-finger chest percussions. I couldn't stop crying. It was the hiccupy kind. Then he wrapped Tinker in a dry washcloth and stuck him on a plate in the oven set on low, thinking it might get him out of shock. When Dad took him out, Tinkerbell was done. My hammy was dead. Mom took Janie home. Death is a buzz-kill for a play-date.

I ran to my room and the solace of my window seat. I did not want to lay on the bed, the scene of the crime. I stared at the sky through the window. The room grew dark. There were no squeaking wheel sounds. I was alone. Soon the stars populated the heavens above the crabapple trees. There was a knock at my door. It was Mom asking me to come out to the dining room for something. I wasn't in the mood for dinner or anything, but I was tired of sitting in the dark.

There, on the dining room table, on the Ethan Allen Lazy Susan, surrounded by candles, was a little coffin that Dad made from a wooden match box, the kind that held matches for lighting the grill. He had elegantly rippled a velvet Crown Royal pouch in the bottom and top. Nestled in the bottom was Tinkerbell with a little flower. There was soft music on the stereo. It was probably Montovani.

That's when Dad recited the 23rd Psalm. Mom and I joined in. "*Yay*, though he *crawls* through the valley of the shadow of death, he shall fear no evil . . ."

I closed the lid and we somberly carried him out to the willow tree, where we buried him.

A few days later, I received a flower arrangement from Dad's secretary with a sympathy card that everyone in his office had signed. It was a really nice thing for them to do. I had never received flowers from an official person in a delivery truck.

The day after that Aunt Vera took me to get another hamster.

THE HOP-TO-IT DIET

My ticket out of poverty has revealed itself. I have discovered the secret to a perfect no-fail exercise regimen. Unlike all the other weight-loss schemes, mine is a true solution that will show results in just two weeks.

This is all you need:

1. A walker/duct tape/tote bag.

2. A pair of crutches. Make sure they are the proper height or you'll kill your shoulders and pits.

3. A really active imagination.

4. Your spouse, partner, or children must move out for a couple weeks so you don't have any help.

5. Shower chair.

Now, imagine that you've had surgery on your foot . . . either foot, although the left may be the best choice because you'll still be able to drive. You won't be able to use your extended medical leave to take off work unless you can convince a physician to lie for you. You must use whatever accrued vacation time you have because "imaginary surgery for the sake of weight loss" will not fly for sick time or short-term disability.

Move your TV to the farthest room from the kitchen.

Keep your phones charged.

Start on a weekend so you get a good jump on it. No pun intended. Since you *haven't* had an actual surgery, you must imagine the very worst consequences for putting weight on the bad foot. Tell yourself that you'll risk permanent disfigurement. Perhaps you can convince yourself that if you touch your foot to the floor you'll be audited on your income tax. Or, if you touch the floor, you'll spend an afterlife in purgatory (do they still have that?). Maybe, like the sidewalk cracks of our youth, if you rest your "bad" foot on the floor someone will break their back. Convince yourself that these consequences are real.

Try to anticipate the things you'll need to put in the bag that you will duct-tape to a walker. The bag will help you transport things from room to room. No matter how much you think it through though, I assure you, you will forget something. But it's FUN when you forget things. It keeps the exercise fresh and challenging!

Any GOOD exercise should be fun . . . right?

VIEW FROM THE LAUNDRY CHUTE

<u>Day One</u>

Get out of bed . . . DON'T put that bad foot down! Grasp the walker, hoist yourself up and hop to the bathroom. Depending on the size of the bathroom, you may have to hop sideways to get in. That's fine; you're just using a different muscle group! Lower yourself to the toilet on one leg while supporting your weight with the walker. This is excellent for the deltoids and forearms. You'll work them when you rise UP from the toilet on one leg as well. You'll have to do this quickly because the phone is ringing in the bedroom. You forgot to put it in your bag! Hop quickly to the bedroom. Now your heart rate is up! Too bad you didn't get to the phone on time. The message indicates it was that cute person you've been hoping would call. Sacrifice is good for the soul.

Now you need to hop back to the bathroom to wash your face and brush your teeth. Are you still on one leg? Goooood. Balance that way while you complete these functions. Good hygiene is important. Work up a good lather so your face is engulfed in soap. This is tricky because balance is a little harder when your eyes are shut.

Oh shoot! The phone is ringing again and you still forgot to put it in the bag. Hop quickly back to the bedroom and worry about rinsing the soap off later. You can't open your eyes to screen the call because the soap is inching its way down your forehead. You answer quickly (heart rate up!), only to have Sears tell you that the warranty on your dryer will expire any day now and it will cost a fortune to fix your machine should you not pay for an extension.

See? Isn't this fun? You've already had a good workout and it's not even an hour into your first day!

Hopefully you have a cat or dog. They've been underfoot all morning because they want food. Hop to the kitchen. Now reach way up or bend down low, on one leg, to get the can of food, wherever you keep it. Hop to the pet dish. Support yourself with one arm on the walker. Still on one foot lower yourself, bending from the waist, to the food dish. Whoops! You're holding the cat/dog food in the hand holding the walker (two fingers on the can, three grasping the walker). You must rise back up, transfer the can to the free hand, and lower yourself back down. Don't touch that "injured" foot to the floor! No cheating! This is GREAT for the abs as well. It's kind of tricky dumping the food into the dish with one hand while the pet is darting in and out, but after dumping the food on his head the first time, you'll figure it out. It only gets better!

Now hop to the bedroom to watch the news. Whew! You've made it to the bed and are already sweating. Settle in, get comfy, and breathe. What have you forgotten? BREAKFAST AND COFFEE!

OK. Take another deep breath. Rise up from the bed on one leg, grasp the walker, and hop back to the kitchen. You may have to zigzag hop across the kitchen floor to get the various items you need to make breakfast and coffee. If you're lucky, your kitchen is only as big as a walk-in closet, like mine. If you have a huge kitchen, bless your heart.

VIEW FROM THE LAUNDRY CHUTE

Stand on one leg while you wait for the coffee to brew. I would suggest you use an insulated, covered coffee mug so that it doesn't splash out when you hop back to the bedroom. You can balance the eggs and toast on a plate in the bag. Now you're cookin'! Hop to the bedroom, lower yourself to the bed. Set your coffee on the end table. Ohhhh, some of your eggs slid off the plate into the bag. No worries! You'll eat half as much! You forgot the salt. You hate eggs without salt. But you sure as hell don't want to hop back to the kitchen. See? You've also lowered your salt intake!

You've earned a nice rest. Just as you begin to doze off, someone pounds on the door. You wake from a stupor, grasp the handles of the walker firmly, make sure there are no exposed body parts, and hop furiously to the front of the house. It's the Jehovah's Witnesses! You forgot they always come on Saturday. They see you're disabled and they want to tell you that Jehovah loves you and will heal you. You say terrible things to them because you are cranky. You hop back toward the bedroom. The dog/cat has peed on the floor sending you shooting across the terrazzo. Now you've worked your GROIN muscles!

You lower yourself to the bed once again, only to realize that you could have put the breakfast dish in the kitchen sink while you were there. Also, you could have cleaned the slimy eggs from the bottom of the bag. You ponder whether to go back. You decide to do it later. You reach for your coffee. It's cold. Shit. You decide to hop back to the kitchen and wash the dish, wipe the bottom of the bag, and nuke your coffee. You slip in the pee again because you forgot about it. You make a mental note to grab some paper towels while you're in the kitchen.

You feel clever because you remembered to put your cell phone in your bag. You prop the coffee cup against the dish. When you get to the kitchen you discover that the coffee leaked into the phone. No worries! You have a cordless that you hear this very minute, ringing back in the bedroom.

You have officially burned 10,000 calories.

You may wish to utilize the crutches when venturing out of the house. No cheating! Keep that foot UP.

If you go to the grocery store you'll find that pushing a cart while using crutches is nearly impossible. You need to use a motorized cart. This is a very humbling experience. To learn humility is a good thing for the soul. You see, this diet is good for the body AND spirit!

Soon you realize that you have to ask people to get things on the top shelf for you. The cart has a basket *half* the size of a regular cart, so you won't be able to get all the food you need. You see how this works? Half the food, half the calories!

The nice young man gets you back to your car and loads the groceries in the trunk. It's been a busy day! You get home, swing your legs out, careful not to touch that foot to the ground. You crutch around to the trunk, open it, and realize that you're not going to be able to carry the heavy bags with both hands on the crutches. Plus, your pet will try to get out when you open the door. It's looking bad

VIEW FROM THE LAUNDRY CHUTE

for the groceries. The neighbors aren't home at the moment. You sure as hell don't want to call someone on your cell phone just to come schlep groceries into the house for you. By the time a neighbor gets home, half of the food has been sitting in the trunk and it's 80 degrees outside. Again, you're cutting down on your food intake! I'm really proud of you at this point for refusing to put that foot down. You left those bags in the trunk! That takes real dedication.

You only have 13 more days of this. Think how many calories you'll burn AT WORK crutching from your desk to the printer 100 times a day. And crutching to and from the cafeteria will burn those lunches like crazy!

By the time you make it through two weeks, you'll have mastered making your hopping trips in the house more efficient. You will anticipate what you need *when* you need it, cutting the trips almost in half. You'll still be burning calories, because you've decided that it's just too much damned trouble to stand on one leg and cook or schlep food in your little bag.

Showers won't get easier, believe me. Backing up to a shower chair and lowering your naked ass to it is always going to be a challenging experience. You will forget to put the soap and towels where you can reach them, but standing up on one leg in a slippery tub is never worth the risk. It's really better for your hair if you skip washing it for several days (all good hair stylists will tell you that), thus limiting your overall shower experiences. The diet is good for your hair as well!

I know I'm on to something here.

Here's an inside tip: buy stock in durable medical equipment because once this diet takes off, walkers and crutches will be flying off the shelves.

THE LAUNDRY CHUTE

The decision to climb into the laundry chute was easy. I was a toddler and an *Alice in Wonderland* fan. If Wonderland could exist through a looking glass and down a rabbit hole, then why not at the bottom of a laundry chute?

My parents shared an old Victorian house in town with another family while our house, out on a rural route, was being completed. The Noll's house had many windows which proved to be a liability when the Jehovah's Witnesses walked up the driveway. They could see when we were home. We had to dive behind overstuffed chairs, hoping we'd not been caught.

The Victorian was a labyrinth of wonderful nooks, window seats, and stairwell hideaways decorated with strange things like a statue of Pan, pillows in various combinations of gingham, hedgehog doorstops, high ceilings, and low windowsills with hand blown glass panes. The Noll's oldest daughter, Phyllis, frequently added to her bug and butterfly collection, so there were interesting displays of them pinned to boards all over the place. She'd find dead birds and bring them in to the kitchen to examine on the table. Her mother loved to bake, so there was always a hint of vanilla in the air. Vanilla and dead birds.

The laundry chute was on the second floor and dropped to the basement, technically making it the third floor. It was tin-lined and square. Without another thought, I crawled in. That afternoon's adventure became a folk legend that was repeated by both our families for years to come. I landed on bare concrete and was rushed to the hospital in one version of the story. Another was that there was only a sheet down there and I was taken to the town doctor who put a bandage over my navel so I would stop crying. I was amazingly unscathed.

As I grew up, I made several decisions that were not thought through and could have caused my untimely demise. I dated a beautiful boy from Yale when I was only sixteen. He was crazy. His idea of a good time was to go out and drive through stop signs. He introduced me to psilocybin, a derivative of mushrooms. We'd go to the local golf course in the dead of winter and make distorted snowmen. We didn't wear coats, boots, or gloves. We were immune to hypothermia.

I decided it would be a good idea when I was seventeen to walk around on a farmhouse roof under the influence of Mickey's Malt and Quaaludes . . . naked.

VIEW FROM THE LAUNDRY CHUTE

I chose to get married in my twenties, mostly because I wanted the gifts. My parents had purchased wedding and shower gifts for half the couples in Canfield. Since my boyfriend and I were moving to Florida, I figured we should get married so I could collect the paybacks that were due us while we still had the chance. We lasted seven years. I still have the Mikasa dinnerware.

Thinking about decisions usually brings me back to the first one I remember . . . the laundry chute. I try to make better choices these days. I stop to think things through. I would never take on a farmhouse roof, naked or otherwise. I definitely do not blow through stop signs. And I wouldn't climb into a laundry chute. I wouldn't fit and I know there is no magic down there, just dirty laundry.

Laundry chutes are kind of like life. Ideas either tank or take off. Choices get up or down votes. Our decisions, good or bad, whether we look up from the abyss or down into it, add dimension to our lives. We have days that are bare concrete landings and days when we end up in fluffy goose-down comforters.

May your landings at least be on a few towels.

AT YOUR OWN RISK

As I drove into the semi-abandoned plaza in Clearwater, Florida in my little Bug, Beetle Bailey, an elderly couple waited to cross from the parking lot to go to the drug store. Being the courteous person I like to think I am, I slowed to a stop. The woman scowled at me and waved me past as if she was swatting away a swarm of killer bees. It was a rigorous dismissal.

Courtesy certainly IS annoying, isn't it? I should have found a nice puddle to whip through and soak those pink polyester pants of hers. Perhaps THAT would put a smile on her face.

This is a frequent occurrence. I have actually been the passEE waiting for a passER to stop so I could cross a parking lot. I'm almost never in a hurry, but I'm always appreciative if someone takes the time to stop for me.

The day I had foot surgery was a different scenario. I was trying to maneuver on crutches while holding my purse. The purse would slide off my shoulder, knocking my hand from the crutch, causing me to hop on one foot while shrugging the purse back up and return the crutch to its normal, upright, under pit, position. I was headed to the drug store for the pain meds I'm so fond of and actually needed for a change. I hobbled slowly, not at all confident on the crutches.

A man in a moving van decided to stop. He angrily waved at me to cross. I mouthed to him, smiling, *no thank you, you go ahead*. Well THAT certainly pissed him off. That I had the nerve to defy a direct order was unacceptable. He rolled down the window and yelled, "JUST GO WILLYA?!" So, being the obedient passive-aggressive person that I am, I smiled sweetly at him, praying I wouldn't topple over while also worrying about the impending curb that loomed ahead. I had to stop for a minute, still dizzy from the anesthesia. The asshole HONKED. Now I wasn't going *fast* enough! I was holding him up! I continued on my way wishing I had telepathic powers so I could cause his transmission to fall out. As it was, I almost wiped out on the curb, at which time that spawn of satan LAUGHED. I bitched about him for a week, extending my hatred to all men for a month.

They are everywhere, these aberrations of humanity. They scorn us for being polite. I believe it has to do with power. These are the Nazis amongst us. That old woman was the Eva Braun to my Jewish merchant riding a donkey. No WAY was she going to cross in front of me at *my* request. She would cross for a finer person than I, or for no one at all. And that truck driver? He WANTED to humiliate me by making me hobble in front of him—even though I was perfectly happy to wait.

When I cross in front of people who stop for me, I always give a little wave and a smile. Inevitably I get exasperated looks as they slouch over their steering wheels as if to say, ya, ya, whatever. Just CROSS already.

Life is complicated when it comes to being civilized . . . I get that. Poor sun-burned Canadians up and down Gulf Boulevard timidly try to cross the street. They come from a country where traffic stops politely for pedestrians. You don't even have to be in a damned crosswalk! There they stand in the median waiting to cross. But it's futile here. No one stops in Pinellas County because they pride themselves on living in a place that has more pedestrian deaths than anywhere else in the country. No Canadian is going to fuck that up. I know people that have been trying to cross Gulf Boulevard for a year and a half now. Loved ones drive by and throw smoked mullet and milkshakes at them so they can keep their strength up.

I SWEAR I've seen people on U.S. 19 speed up when people a block away are running terrified across the highway. They go even faster if it's a family.

Will I continue to stop for people? Yes. Even though I'm willing to bet my life they will sometimes yell at me for doing so.

UNDER THE TABLE

He handed me the brown paper bag under the table. My palms were sweaty as I glanced around with trepidation to see if anyone in the room had noticed. The product was tightly wrapped in cellophane within the bag. I couldn't believe that of all the things I'd tried in my fifty-plus years, I'd never tried *this*.

I felt ashamed and ridiculous. I wondered if I was having some kind of a mid-life issue. (I realized that by placing this experience in a mid-life category I'd have to live to be one hundred and fourteen.)

Still, there I was, accepting the goods under the table. It was lighter than I expected. I hoped it wouldn't crumble and somehow escape from the bag into my purse. I wondered if it could be detected by dogs.

That evening, I carefully unwrapped it. At that point I still wasn't sure I'd actually *ingest* it. There, on my kitchen table, slightly to the left of the Alcatraz salt and pepper shakers, they lay.

Two large squares of matzo.

Oh hell, I thought. *Just do it.*

I bit off a corner of one of the crackers. It was kind of bland. It reminded me of a saltine without the salt. I began to think of ways to experiment with it. Soup was too obvious. Butter... too boring. Jelly? Jelly just seemed WRONG.

My bachelor-food-mind kicked in. Bachelor food is food you throw together based simply on cravings. It takes less than five minutes to create this type of cuisine. It provides instant gratification. Bachelor food should be eaten while standing at the kitchen sink or lying in bed. It's the first food that appeals to you when you open the cupboard or fridge. It's not terribly healthy stuff. It's also *not* food you serve to other people because it's your *own* intimate craving.

I placed the matzo on a paper plate and shmeered it with olive tapenade. Then, I drizzled Hunan hot pepper oil over it. I placed thinly sliced provolone on top. Everything's better with cheese. I popped it in the microwave. Bachelor food generally involves a microwave.

I decided to take it to bed, I was *that* attracted to it.

Oh MAN, it was GOOD. It was WAY good. My endorphins were all over the place and my pupils, I'm sure, were dilated. I didn't even care about the mess. It WAS messy. GOD, was it messy. The cat was disgusted and took his leave.

There is still a stain on the sheets.

I've added matzo to my grocery list. I don't care who sees it anymore.

It's out of the bag.

AUTUMN OF 1967

In the autumn of 1967, after The Summer of Love, my dad successfully prevented a racial conflict. I had threatened to stab a Black man. I was eleven.

I was a naive and innocent child who didn't know much beyond grade school and my house in the outskirts of Canfield, Ohio, population 4,997. We lived at the end of a long driveway that took us to a rural highway frequented by eighteen-wheelers. My best friends were a boy named Howdy and a willow tree.

My brother Jimmy had earned scholarships for academics as well as football. He was accepted at Rutgers University. Pretty good for a Canfield kid. While he was earning scholarships, I was earning nickels, dimes, and occasionally, quarters selling merchandise from my yellow Radio Flyer wagon. It was red when it was new. My dad got it used, sanded the rust off, and painted it.

The summer of '67, while Jim was getting ready for his second year at Rutgers, I continued my door-to-door route to the neighbor's houses, dragging my wagon through ditches and over hilly lawns and long fields. I sold handmade greeting cards, fortunes written on strips of paper, rolled up, and placed in empty pill capsules ... the contents of which had been dumped in Mom's pansies. I sold drugged pansies. I sold wooden ice cream spoons decorated with broken glass from marbles that I smashed with a hammer, my first crude attempt at mosaic.

That fall, Dad decided we would go on a road trip to visit my brother in New Brunswick, New Jersey, population 41,885. We were going to see a football game during the visit, even though Jim didn't play that year. Mom and I loaded the trunk. Grandma went with us, too. Grandma and Grandpa had a farm up the road from us. Grandpa stayed behind to tend to the animals, and I closed my door-to-door business, at least until spring. The neighbors were probably relieved.

We arrived in New Jersey, resplendent with red and gold maple trees and a little snap in the air that made me think of cold apple cider. Dad found a motel where the four of us would share a room. After we unpacked, we drove to Rutgers. The campus was crowded with colorful trees, green lawns, and big red brick buildings with beautiful façades, some with Roman pillars. We saw a statue of a man named William the Silent. He held a book under one arm and the other was raised above his head, finger pointing to the sky. There was a beer can on it.

We pulled up to a big, old, white house with a huge porch across the front and a bunch of letters above the entrance that said

VIEW FROM THE LAUNDRY CHUTE

Phi Gamma Delta followed by funny symbols. This was where Jimmy lived with a bunch of other guys.

After a brief tour of the campus, we went to the football game. We climbed the bleachers and chose the first row behind a section of Black people. I'd seen very few people of color in my short life. I figured they must be in a club or something. Maybe like our Glee Club at school. I went in first, then Mom, Grandma, Jim and Dad. Dad needed the end seat so he could stick his stiff leg in the aisle. In the Army, they didn't have knee replacement surgery when you had a bad knee injury. They either cut your leg off or fused it so it was stiff.

Mom dug around in her purse to get the postcard of Nixon playing piano with his daughter Tricia. On the back was a note written to me that said, "Debbie, Thank you for your nice letter. Richard Nixon." She had been showing that postcard to everyone. She was so proud of it. She handed it to Grandma so she could pass it down to Jim.

I wrote letters to lots of people, Everett Dirksen, Barry Goldwater, Nixon, William F. Buckley, and Joy Adamson to name a few. I was a good little Republican. I didn't know whether Joy Adamson was a Republican or not. I wrote to her because of *Born Free*, her book about Elsa the lion. Besides, I had no idea what it meant to be a Republican anyway. My parents were, so it had to be a good thing.

It was time for the National Anthem so we all stood with our hands over our hearts. Well, not ALL of us stood. That whole section of Black people stayed seated. They had their heads down with gloved fists in the air. I thought it was neat, but also confusing . . . had someone died? When we sat down, Mom said, "Well that just makes me sick, not standing for our country's national anthem. I'm just sick!"

Right about this time, the postcard was making its way back to our end of the bench. Just as Mom reached for it, the Black man in front of us snatched it and passed it to his friends who took turns reading it and laughing. The man leaned back and looked at my mom.

"You sick, lady? You feelin' bad?"

He yelled to the people he was sitting with.

"Anyone got some aspirin? We got a sick lady here!"

"Well it just makes me sick that you won't stand for the anthem," Mom said. Then she started to cry. I never saw my mom cry before. A Black woman with big round hair gave Mom the crumpled postcard.

I leaned forward and said to the man, "If I had a knife, I'd STAB you."

"Would you, little girl? What d' you s'pose would happen to you, little girl? What d'you s'pose the POlice would do to you? You think they throw you in jail? What you s'pose the POlice would do to ME?"

"They wouldn't do ANYTHING to you because they'd be AFRAID of you! They'd put ME in JAIL!" I was furious. We were face to face. He looked amused.

VIEW FROM THE LAUNDRY CHUTE

While this exchange was happening, Dad was sideways walking down the row as fast as he could with a stiff leg. It was more like a side-step-hop-side-step-hop. When he got to me he hoisted me up and toted me back to where my brother was sitting, thus interrupting a conflict that I was willing to continue in defense of Mom.

After the game, my parents bought me and Grandma sandwiches and chips to eat in the motel while they went out. I'm sure they needed a few drinks. Grandma put Lawrence Welk on TV. We propped ourselves up in the bed. As she ate her chips, licking her fingers between bites, she said in a very smug . . . no, almost playful tone,

"Did you hear what that big darky said to you?"

"Huh?"

"He said he was going to find you and kill you."

She took a bite of her sandwich, winked at me, then turned to watch TV.

I hadn't heard the man say anything like that, after all, I was the one who'd threatened murder. I suspected that Grandma made it up. I checked the lock on the door anyway.

For years I wondered why she said that to me, and the way she said it. I knew she used the word "darky" when referring to Black people. Around our house we said "colored" in the sixties. Not much better. But she was a farmer. She had strange words for lots of things. She worked her fields with Black people who came over from

Youngstown to make extra money. She would make a big meal for everyone after the work was done.

Grandma wasn't a mean woman by nature. She always made a fuss over us. I don't recall hearing her disparage other races or very many other people until a reporter got her age wrong in the town paper when they wrote about how many years she'd attended the county fair. She's probably STILL pissed, wherever she is.

I concluded, after years of thinking about that day, that Grandma was probably trying to scare me so I would not do something stupid like that again. It was her way to teach me a lesson, even though it was a fucked-up way to do it. My mouth still gets me in trouble when my temper flares.

Funny thing, though. That incident didn't make me afraid of Black people. You'd think that what she'd told me so cavalierly all those years ago would have influenced me. I'm glad it didn't.

STILETTOS AND MT. McKINLEY

I remember standing behind Carol Mahoney in high school gym class. She was supposed to run and spring off a slanted board, as is the method for encountering what is called a "pommel horse." Two spotters stood impotently on either side of the large, ugly leather thing that reminded me of a meat loaf and stood approximately three or four feet from the safety of the shiny, wooden floor. Two iron handles jutted from the top in the center of it. We were each, in turn, supposed to spring from the board, grasp the handles, and swing our legs, stuck firmly together, sideways over the monstrosity.

Carol gave one of those little hopping starts, ran toward the big meat loaf, sprang from the board, and promptly broke her leg. We're talking exposed bone jutting from flesh.

I was so relieved. The chaos that ensued assured that I would NOT have to be next.

I didn't see the value of such things as flinging oneself through the air on hanging rings or slamming a gut into parallel bars, uneven or otherwise, or doing a flip on top of a beam that was about six inches wide. So I flat-out refused to participate. I believe I told Mrs. Saunders, "There's NO fucking WAY I'm doing that shit."

I failed gym.

I spent a great deal of time visiting with the principal, a well-respected man who was also the football coach, and who, years later, was busted for porn on his computer.

The last year I went to Camp Whitewood, a place for 4-H nerds, we'd hiked on a trail that required scaling a flat rock approximately six feet high. The camp counselors stood at the top, grasped our hands, and pulled us up . . . except me. They tried. But the idea of being pulled up a piece of flat rock scared me half to death. They had both of my hands but I let go with one so I could cover my eyes. I spun around and slammed my back against the rock and hung there, grasped by one arm, and cried. The counselor, I think his name was Tom, finally had to let me go. I slid about a foot to the mossy forest floor.

I had a similar experience on a camping trip to Cooks Forest in Pennsylvania. My parents took a large portion of the immediate family to the beautiful primordial forest. We brought my friend Diane and my sister's father–in-law, who was about 80. We decided to hike the River Trail, a pleasant walk along the gorge.

VIEW FROM THE LAUNDRY CHUTE

Someone decided that it would be funny to turn the rustic sign to the left, basically sending people down the side of the hill towards the raging river, rather than along the smooth path that ran safely (and levelly) above. Everyone, including my parents, the 80-year-old man, and my friend Diane, took it all in stride and climbed down the hill. My father had a stiffened leg from the Army, so was basically operating on only one good leg. My mother, who was even less athletic than me, climbed down the hill as if she was going to the mall to buy shoes.

I clung to a tiny sapling on the side of the mountain and cried. My friend Diane sprinted up and down the slope to show me how easy it was. My Dad invoked the name of Jeezus H. Kriste while yelling up at me to pull myself together, let go, and slide down on my butt.

I know there are people who can do amazing and totally unnatural things with their bodies. God bless those people. I have the utmost respect for folks who are compelled to climb sheer, treacherous, mountains of rock even though there is an excruciatingly high mortality rate.

This brings me to the purpose of this story. High heels.

I truly, TRULY, do not know how women walk in heels. To me, they may as well climb Mt. McKinley. Why would anyone place themselves in such peril? There are stones, rocks, gaping wooden slats, slippery tiled floors, sand, dirt, and curbs. How is it possible to walk in shoes that are not only made with a skinny, six inch stiletto, but the toe is pointed and the whole damned shoe is constructed on a three inch platform? How do women and drag queens walk in these? WHY do they walk in these?

Let's examine the similarities of climbing mountains and walking in high heels.

Mountains:

- Climbing at a high altitude can cause nausea and dizziness due to thin air. Eyelids may swell and ooze pus.
- You can experience red, tender, cracked, scabbed, and bleeding skin.
- You can develop intense cramps accompanied with diarrhea.
- The lower calf can become swollen and painful with a pale, or even bluish, cast. This could be indicative of a clot (or thrombophlebitis).
- You can plummet to your death.

Heels:

- In heels the air is thinner up there, too.
- Bones can shatter like toothpicks when the ankle juts to the side after an encounter with a curb or an errant stone.
- The stress of wearing heels can cause diarrhea.
- Your eyelids can swell and ooze pus after falling face first into an ant mound.

VIEW FROM THE LAUNDRY CHUTE

- You can plummet to your death.

I have read that for every fraction of an inch you add to the heel of your shoe, the rest of your body has to compensate in order to remain upright. Bone structure, posture, and core muscle strength have everything to do with how a body reacts to stilettos. Based on this, it stands to reason that permanent disfigurement will occur for the stiletto wearer. One begins to resemble the Elephant Man by the time she reaches sixty.

Physicians have found that wearing high heels for any length of time increases the normal forward curve of the back to an exaggerated curve and causes the pelvis to tip forward in an ABNORMAL way. Oooooooh, SEXY. They also say that the pounds of pressure placed on the ball of a foot in a high-heeled shoe is about the same as carrying a baby hippo around on your shoulder. I would gladly carry a baby hippo if it needed a ride, but I'm pretty sure it's physically impossible. Yet, stiletto wearers are essentially doing that very thing.

High heel wearers' calf muscle fibers are 13% shorter than those of women who wear flat shoes. Women and drag queens have to have their calves stretched on a primitive rack prior to going to the beach in flip-flops.

Kudos to the people who have climbed Mount McKinley or even a rock wall at the gym, or a mound of gravel down by the railroad tracks. And Kudos to the people who can maneuver the wooden slats at the Palm Pavilion on a sandy beach on a crowded Saturday night in their six-inch stilettos.

I'm thinking it's better to climb Mt. McKinley.

I've tried wearing heels and can't make it from point A to point B. I'm sure as hell not going to attempt to climb a mountain in them. Not that I ever suggested in this story that anyone should attempt to climb a damned mountain in heels. I'm just saying.

DEAR GOD

Dear God, Jesus, and the Virgin Mary,

I know we're never supposed to ask You Guys for stuff, especially money, even though football players regularly pray for wins, and *those* guys have big houses and enough money for lawyers and bail. Jeezus! You'd think that would be enough!

But we *are* allowed to pray for forgiveness. So I'm asking You to forgive me because I want to win The Publisher's Clearinghouse Sweepstakes, also known as P.C. I would be ever so grateful if you would let me win *just once.*

They continually send envelopes full of advertisements so I have to spend an hour finding the special stamps that must be included on the entry forms. I know P.C. does this because they want us to order stuff, but I never did because they assured me that it wouldn't affect my chances of winning. They *say* I can still win 10,000 dollars a week for life just by returning my entries with the official labels and elusive special stamps. I think I'm long overdue to win because of the money I've spent on postage over the years. You have to *pay* to send those back!

This year I decided I would actually order something just in case it would give me an edge. P.C. used to offer this neat Toe Spreader that alleviates bunion pain while you sleep. So I decided I would order one for my sister.

See? I do nice things for people! But to my dismay, they didn't offer it this year. I looked through every stupid insert three times. No Toe Spreader!

I do not need Amish Wood Polish. Don't get me wrong, I love the Amish and I'm sure their polish is top notch. I am blessed to own several things made of wood. Not everyone has wooden things, and for that I am grateful . . . not that others don't have wooden things, but that *I* do, just to be clear. Still, I don't think I need Amish Wood Polish.

I also don't want a Scrabble Word Dictionary with extra-large type. I don't have much time for games, and I have no one to play with. Besides, isn't it cheating to look up the words? But I *could* play Scrabble if I really wanted to, because I am blessed to be able to play games fairly well and I know lots of words. I don't even require extra-large type because I can still see, and for that I am truly blessed. I thank You Guys for these abilities. Really. But it would be a waste for me to order a Scrabble Dictionary and I'm not a wasteful person most of the time.

VIEW FROM THE LAUNDRY CHUTE

I don't need a Nose Hair Trimmer or Socks That Grip the Floor when you walk. Yet.

I don't need the Cooking Measurements Conversion chart that sticks to the fridge, or the handy Sharpening Stone for Ninja Knives that P.C. also offers. I don't cook. But I *can* cook reasonably well when I really want to, so for that I am very blessed. I mean, I know people that can't even boil an EGG properly. I'm not disparaging those people, I *swear*.

Which reminds me, I also don't need the Tiny Teflon Skillet in which to cook a single egg. I mean, it's not like one egg gets lost on a medium-sized skillet.

Frankly, I can't see why anyone would want a Jesus Saves magnetic ribbon for their car. I mean "Jesus Saves" is an important message, don't get me wrong. But I think most Christians already believe that Jesus and God and the Virgin Mary are probably proficient savers. Everyone else might read that magnet and get a little pissed that only Jesus saves, which implies that Buddha and Mohammed and L. Ron Hubbard don't.

And who needs a Battery-Operated, Miniature Plastic Dune Buggy for crissakes?

So it looks like I won't be ordering anything again this year, which is why I really need Your help.

If You could find it in Your celestial hearts to let me win, please make sure the Publishers Clearinghouse people do not come to the front door, but rather, to the door in the carport. And make sure they come on a day when I'm home and I've bathed.

    Amen.

THIS IS YOUR BRAIN AT FUNERALS

When I was eleven, Grandma Grindle sent me down to the strawberry patch to get Grandpa Grindle for supper. He told me he'd be up in a minute.

Up at the house, as we passed around a platter of corn on the cob, a stranger knocked at the door. He said there was a man lying in the field. We rushed down to find Grandpa lying on his side across three rows of plants. He was a tall man. I began to cry but Mom told me to stop because it would upset Grandma. It turned out that Grandma was more concerned about supper getting cold.

Grandpa Grindle had bought me a gold-plated charm bracelet with little pieces of wood dangling from it at Rogers Farm Market. He took me there often. I wanted to wear it to his funeral but Mom said it didn't match my dress.

I'd never seen a dead person before. I'd only experienced dead pets. My hamster Tinkerbell died prematurely because I accidently sat on the poor little guy. We buried him under the willow tree with all my other deceased creatures. A few years ago the people who lived in the house had the tree removed. I wish I had known. I would have re-located the bodies.

I stood there by that big box and stared at Grandpa. I wondered why he had his glasses on. I heard my aunt Vera tell cousin Kathy, who was also suffering from "funeral brain," to walk up and put her arm around me. I could hear Kathy's shoes clicking behind me. She dropped her arm across my shoulders like a train-crossing gate. I started to laugh . . . really hard.

When I tried to stop I made a funny, squealing sound. Tears streamed down my face. I bit the inside of my mouth until it bled. Kathy steered me to a bench outside where I laughed for at least another ten minutes. I have no idea why.

When Dad died we had a nice memorial service in the church that he and Mom had attended.

The Masons sent a guy that recited a special ceremony for members who pass away. He went on for almost an hour. That's a lot of stuff for someone to know by heart. Then my brother got up and told a really funny story about mowing yards that illustrated the kind of work-ethic our Dad had. Jimmy didn't get paid for the jobs because

VIEW FROM THE LAUNDRY CHUTE

Dad just figured it was something a person was supposed to do to help other people. Jimmy did not share this philosophy.

My sister talked about taking the car when she wasn't supposed to, then running it through the back of the garage. I was planning to tell my favorite Dad story about scaring him in the middle of the night by shaking him and saying that I had something *really important* to discuss. He shot out of bed. I assume he thought I was going to tell him I was pregnant. But I only wanted to buy a llama coat from a hippie shop in Youngstown and I needed permission to take the money out of my savings. He said, "Buy the damned coat!"

Instead of the coat story, I inexplicably announced to my parents' huge church family, and the Shriners, that I had no faith and probably never would. This is not true. But I said it. Everyone stared at me. I tried to back-pedal by assuring everyone that at least DAD had faith, but by then it was no use. I was afraid of what *else* might come out of my mouth involuntarily, like the F-word or something . . . so I went back to my seat. Luckily, Mom was sufficiently confused by then to not notice. She was the only one that didn't.

It really pissed me off, in retrospect, when my friend's dad passed away a month later and I did a really good job on *his* eulogy. I actually said exactly what I wanted to say for *him*. But I'd made an ass of myself for *my* dad.

We had a kind of lame memorial service for Mom. It seemed like a good idea at the time to have it at the adult living facility where she passed away, because most of her friends at the church where Dad's service was were gone. It was also two hours away.

Throughout Mom's memorial, some of the residents yelled out if there would be food, or they'd ask each other who Phyllis was.

My brother pulled through with yet another humorous and poignant eulogy that had us all in tears. My sister read some of the memoir she wrote, but unfortunately went on for several more pages than we expected. I don't think she knew how to stop. The residents became restless. I got up and told an amusing, short story about Mom's mink stole and how she wore it to my Animal Charity League dinner. The story went well. Just as I was about to sit down, I saw my sister wildly motioning toward my daughter. I mouthed, "What?"

She mouthed, "Talk about KRISTIN."

I had no idea what to say. I wanted to say that my parents took her on fun summer vacations. But I proceeded to tell everyone that I did not raise my daughter, my parents did. Again, I was saying something that was not true. I went on to say that, had they not taken her on trips and done the things they had for her, she would *not* be the wonderful person she had become. Then I sat down. My daughter looked at me as if I had drool running out of my mouth.

The Hospice minister came up to me after the service and asked if my parents raised Kristin because I had had a drug or alcohol problem. My daughter yelled at the Hospice minister, "It's none of your fucking business. Go AWAY."

VIEW FROM THE LAUNDRY CHUTE

I *did* raise my daughter. I have no idea why I said that my parents did. I might as well have told everyone that she was raised by wolves. It would have sounded just as strange.

For some reason my brother has been immune to "funeral brain" when he gets up to speak. Maybe it's because he attended Toastmasters.

I believe something becomes rearranged in our brains when we mourn. Come to think of it, it's not really limited to funerals, but any place where a solemn demeanor is appropriate.

When my sister and I visited our parents years ago in Sebring, we went to Sunday worship at their church. It was a brand new church with folding chairs with rubber cushions. There were no pews yet.

Mom was in the choir. She was so excited to see her girls *attending church* that she pointed us out to everyone around her as we took our seats next to Dad.

Presbyterians stand and sit a LOT. Every time the congregation sat down it sounded like a chorus of whoopee cushions. From the corner of my eye I could see my sister's shoulders shaking. I began to laugh loudly. Biting the inside of my mouth didn't work. I had to run outside and collapse against the side of the Fellowship Hall in fits of hysterical laughter.

Dad poured cocktails when we got home. It was close enough to noon for a much-needed happy hour.

Maybe "funeral brain" is God playing a joke on us in an attempt to take our minds off of being too sad. *I'll just damage part of the frontal lobe down by the pituitary gland for a while. It'll be a HOOT. Ha!*

I can understand what you're trying to do God, I really can. And I appreciate Your sense of humor. But I think You should stick to what You're *really* good at, like babies, trees, and thunder.

Or just make my *brother* screw up at the next funeral.

GETTING PICKY ABOUT AGING

I used to sit on my brother's back when I was small. There was a bottle of rubbing alcohol and box of Kleenex within reach. They were my surgical tools. I took the process seriously.

My job was to get the zits on his back. He was fifteen, I was seven. I suppose this is how we bonded. I enjoyed it when he screamed in pain as I applied the alcohol liberally to a freshly squeezed zit. He'd writhe around but I never fell off. I suppose this was as much fun as a little kid way out in rural Anytown could have, unless long hours sitting atop a dog house counted.

I enjoyed clipping my Dad's fingernails when we drove along the highway during summer vacations. He'd swing his arm over the front seat of the car so I could work on his nails from the back seat. He liked it when I pushed the cuticles back and clipped the nails ACROSS, not *rounded.* We'd barrel down the turnpike, pre-Nader seatbelts, pre-fifty-five miles an hour speed limits, hauling a Banner trailer, while I snipped away with a Swiss Army clipper.

This is the same dad who argued bitterly with my daughter when he'd take her out to practice driving.

"Keep BOTH hands on the wheel at ten and two," he'd yell when she casually handled the steering wheel with both hands at the bottom.

"Ten and TWO!"

"Stop YELLING Pop-Pop! I know what I'm doing! JEEZUS. Chill OUT!"

"If you don't want to hold the wheel at TEN and TWO, then *pull over!*"

She did just that and the two of them didn't speak for the rest of the evening. Fucking Leos.

I didn't work on his left hand until we set up camp for the night. We'd play a couple rounds of Jarts, which were pointy-assed metal spears with huge plastic "feathers" on the other end. The object was to toss them through the air and stick them within plastic circles that lay flat on the ground . . . a medieval twist on horseshoes. The fact that I have both eyes and all my toes is a miracle.

This brings me to the purpose of the story.

My deterioration.

I liken my older body to those zits and fingernails of my youth. It's a contrast of emotions, both disgusting and mesmerizing, appalling and interesting.

VIEW FROM THE LAUNDRY CHUTE

For example, when I look at myself in the mirror every morning I can absolutely swear my neck has come farther forward from where it used to be. The skin below my jaw, in what is commonly known as "the neck area," has become more and more like the shirred fabric on the side of a bad prom dress. A profile view reveals skin from my chin reaching straight down to my chest, very similar to that of a pelican. I use magic creams that are supposed to tighten the jawline for fifteen minutes. I try not to allow *anyone* to see me from the side. This is not easy to accomplish. It's exhausting.

There was this guy? Who took my picture from the side? And posted it on Facebook? They've never found his body. Ugly doesn't mean *stupid*, ladies and gentlemen.

My legs are the approximate color of wallpaper paste. The purple spider veins around my ankles look like a bad tattoo rendering of bare trees in the winter. I swear there's a new branch every day. Some of the "branches" end in purple splotches, as if the ink got clogged then suddenly spit out a glob. The spiders strive to become varicose. I know this because they whisper at night and tell me. They scare the cat. Still, I find them terrifyingly interesting. Like watching a boil develop.

There is an actual bulge midway up the back of my left leg, like the gnarl on a tree.

My arms are another source of introspection and alarm. In high school I was voted *the person with the most beautiful arms and back.*

Recently, I found a cool cotton shift in a Tibetan boutique in San Francisco. It had ruffles around the neck. I tried it on. I saw the gamine I *used* to be, in my imagination, because the mirror was too high for me to get a true body shot. I thought it would look really sweet with tights and black, patent leather Mary Janes or Swedish clogs. When I came out of the dressing room, my daughter, ever the diplomat, said, "Mommy, why don't you try the two-toned gray dress *without* the ruffle around the neck?" I didn't listen.

When I returned home, I examined my mirrored image with the discerning eye of a zit-picker. I looked like a large tranny in the thing. My meaty biceps burst forth from the armholes beneath the ridiculous ruffles.

There isn't much to say about my breasts, except that they grow longer each day. I plan to wrap them around what's left of my neck to keep me warm this winter—a *boob boa*, if you will.

My stomach is far more interesting than all the other parts combined.

When I tried on clothes in the Last Chance Thrift Store my eyes were drawn to the entity that is planning to separate from my body and take over the world after feeding for a couple more months on its host. Such pastiness and ripples I haven't seen since Ghostbusters! I don't need to tell you to what I'm referring. I stood in that musty place and stared into the chipped mirror as I lifted the thing that bulged from my front and dropped it, testing the gravity of the situation. It could actually be draped over my forearm like a small blanket or cat. I wondered if I could sell it. Could it be varnished and used as an end table? How much would it cost to remove?

There wasn't much air in that little fitting room. The smell of moldy things was causing me to hallucinate. I stuffed the bulge back into my jeans.

I don't have the time I'd need to fascinate you about the paper-thin quality of my skin, and the fact that it occasionally decides to bleed profusely in the oddest places merely because I've leaned against something or scratched an itch.

I find that my body has become like a science experiment. There's a cosmic nerd down the hallway of my life, just past the ladies' room, in Lab 101, who grows things in petri dishes to apply to my sleeping form at night.

I can't wait to see what changes are in store for tomorrow.

I really need to trim these nails.

I AM CURIOUS (CHEESEBURGER)

I sat in a quaint beach bistro in a quaint beach town that was *way* out of my quaint comfort zone. I tend to stay within a ten-mile radius unless someone else is driving. It was hot and I wore jeans. There were women in bikinis all around me. I resolved to leave as soon as I finished my Corona if the blind date didn't show.

I was there to meet an Australian named Frank. We met online. I was just curious, really. I wasn't looking for a husband. The only way I would actually live with a man long-term would be if it were in a big house with two separate wings and a calendar in the middle on which we could schedule meetings.

Frank arrived before I finished my beer, before I could escape. We checked each other out.

"You don't look like your pictures," he said. "How recent are they?"

VIEW FROM THE LAUNDRY CHUTE

I thought it an unusual thing to say for an icebreaker. Usually people start with things like, "Did you have trouble getting here?" or "Isn't the weather gorgeous, though I hear it might rain," or "Nice to meet you. I'm [name here]."

"One picture was taken this past Christmas, and the other two were taken in April." I said.

He squinted at me as he rummaged through his pockets for a cigarette.

"It's funny how people can look so different in a picture," he mumbled as he lit his cigarette.

"Are you saying I should post new pictures?"

"No, darlin', I'd go with the ones you got."

He winked and punched me in the arm as I took note of the fact that he had no ass and a person could hang-glide in the deep wrinkles of his face. We hadn't talked for more than ten minutes before he ordered the second of about ten pints he'd have before I'd extricate myself from the evening.

There were moments when I actually *almost* liked him. He had lived all over the world. He had a great accent. He paid for my cheeseburger and beer.

He continued to order beer for me that I did not drink because I could barely get through the second one. Wine is my poison but I decided to go with beer so I wouldn't drink too much. Sweating beer bottles stood around my plate like little soldiers waiting to be called into action.

I sat facing the water. He faced the back of the patio where other people were seated at tall, square, metal tables. We perched on high iron chairs that were impossible to move up *to* or away *from* the table. They were almost tall enough for a nose-bleed. A trip to the bathroom proved a challenge. I had to sort of "tip" myself sideways until my foot touched the deck. I could then, using both hands, maneuver the chair away from me.

Dark clouds gathered on the horizon. The wind whipped around us. There was lightning off in the distance. I thought about people who were hit by lightning on cloudless, sunny beaches. I suggested it might be a good idea to wrap up the evening so I could get home. He ordered two more beers. I silently said a prayer to God so that She wouldn't let me die of electrocution with that man.

I could tell that Frank was not a person who liked people. Let me clarify. He didn't like *fat* people. Had I had an inkling of this during the first half of the date when he was almost sober, I would have left. But there I was, the victim of a cheeseburger with fries. It was a good cheeseburger. I hadn't eaten all day.

"OH MY GAWD!" he shouted, "Turn around and get a look at THAT. That girl's ARSE is literally SPILLING over the sides of her chair. She has thighs bigger than my whole body!" He lifted up his shirt to prove it. "I go to the gym four days a week, darlin'. Go ahead, touch me stomach . . . *touch* it. You'd never know I was sixty!"

I did not touch his stomach. I was mortified.

61

VIEW FROM THE LAUNDRY CHUTE

"TURN AROUND, I SAY, and look at how bloody fat she is!"

I leaned over the table and hissed at him, "I will NOT. What's the matter with you?"

"That girl can't (pronounced kont) be more than twenty. She'll be DEAD before she's thirty." He said this as he threw back another pint and lit a cigarette.

"Oh, I see. You're *concerned* about her. You *care* about her. Am I right?" I pictured him in a shroud about to be dumped from the side of a boat.

He gave me a look as if this hadn't occurred to him but it was a good angle to take so he'd go with it. "Well of course I care about the poor thing. Now just swing 'round and take a gander!"

I felt ill. I couldn't get away fast enough.

"I have to go now, Frank. Thank you so much for the beer and burger. I want to get out of here before the storm comes."

He grabbed my arm. "I thought we could get some coffee and I could show you the view from me condo. All these blokes here know me." He swept his arm from one side of the place to the other in a grand gesture. "I'm not a *rapist*. I just want to show you the damned view and have some bloody coffee. These mates will tell you I'm a nice enough guy."

I yanked my arm away and reminded him of the many headlines that read, *Body Parts Found in Back Yard. Neighbors Say Killer Was a Nice Guy.*

When I got home, I emailed him that I am not the woman for him because I actually LIKE people he would consider fat. I like all shapes and sizes of people. I don't give a rat's ARSE about six pack abs that disguise ugly people, or even six pack abs on *nice* people. It's the stuff on the *inside* of the wrapper that delights me; the melted goodness, the salt, the flavor of a person's spirit.

And by the way, thanks for the cheeseburger.

HANDLE WITH CARE

There is a Patty Griffin song titled "Be Careful." These are not profound words. These are words that are uttered, more often than not, as a gentle warning. They're really more about concern than warning. For instance, you may remind a co-worker as they leave to be careful. It's not an angry mandate like *Get away from there! Leave me alone! Don't touch that!* It's a simple *be careful*, full of care . . . take care.

The song is about all the girls, all *us* girls, from everywhere. The refrain in the song is, *be careful with me.* In a moment of inspiration, years ago, I decided that I wanted those words tattooed to my back.

You're rolling your eyes now. Let me explain. I've spent so much time in hospitals and nursing facilities with my parents and friends to know that being *careful* is sometimes forgotten amidst the changing of dressings, the hanging of bags, insertion of IVs, and the lifting of the body up, down, and over. The infirm become merely anonymous objects with bodily functions ... functions that require attention.

I believe a gentle reminder is in order.

You may think that *be careful with me* would be the inspiration for a different scenario. You would be wrong. I won't lie to you, it *did* cross my mind. However, the naughty implication is *far* less likely than the nursing home of my not-too-distant-future. This was the state of my mind when the idea came to me like a germ. It grew like a virus. Only one thing held me back, the cold unadulterated fear of needles.

My daughter has approximately seventeen tattoos at last count. I've even accompanied her on one occasion as she read a magazine while they carved another image on her skin. She winced occasionally.

I polled everyone I saw who had a tattoo. "What did it FEEL like?" I asked. The answers varied from a constant bee sting, to a really bad sunburn. Once the answer was, "Well, if you made it through childbirth, you can make it through a tattoo." Great.

I screamed like a banshee for eleven hours and begged for drugs when I birthed my daughter. They had to scrape her out of me. I felt like a pumpkin being carved for Halloween. The concept of "pushing," as the nurse and doctor asked of me, was totally incomprehensible. I puffed my neck out like a Bearded Dragon. This was not the region from which they needed me to push. If getting a tattoo was only like this, I would probably abandon the idea.

VIEW FROM THE LAUNDRY CHUTE

Still, my possible tattoo nagged at me. I had nightmares of lying on a steel table with my arms strapped down in restraints, and a sound not unlike a chainsaw getting closer. I scream and twitch only to have these horrible, jagged, black marks on my body for the rest of my life.

When I went to visit my daughter, the Coolest Person I Know in Atlanta, I was surrounded by twenty-somethings with boundless energy when they finally got up around two in the afternoon. *Their* schedule was to be *my* schedule for the next four days. My kid dragged me around town from three in the afternoon until four in the morning. I have never known a better docent for anything counter-culture. But that's another story.

We drove down Ponce de Leon, but you don't call it that when you're cool and live in Atlanta. You simply call it Ponce.

Kristin said, "That's where I got a couple of mine." She pointed to a place called Liberty Tattoos.

"I want to get one." It was time. She asked me if I was sure. I took a Xanax and said I was. So she pulled into the lot and told me to wait while she checked to see if her friend had time to "do me." I sat in her car for what seemed like hours sifting through books, trash, and thrift store finds, until she came back to tell me he had an opening. He had time.

"Hey everyone, this is my mom. She's getting her *first* tattoo." Polite disinterest shifted my way. Her friend was busy torturing a young man's shoulder, but he smiled the sweetest smile and had the kindest eyes. He told me it was nice to meet me. He pointed toward a table with his skin-drill. He told me I should look through the books to get an idea of what font I wanted. I knew he was a good choice for my first time.

Be Careful with me was going to ride along my lower back for the rest of my life, so the script had to be feminine but not fancy, because it needed to be legible for all of the nursing home aides who would be flipping me over in the future.

He checked his schedule.

"Damn!" he said. "I forgot that someone is coming after this guy. Maybe your mom could come back at nine?" The Xanax had just kicked in. I knew I would chicken out by nine if I had to think about it for a few hours. He suggested another artist and assured me that this person was a very good artist. I reluctantly agreed. Man-with-kind-eyes disappeared into a back room.

Soon, another man emerged rubbing his eyes. He looked like a felon. I imagined him to be the wiry, mean guy that the other felons don't mess with. It appeared he'd been disturbed from a nap. He was entirely covered with tattoos all the way to the top of his head. I could tell he didn't give a rat's ass that I was someone's silly mother in a mid-life crisis there to get her first tattoo. I took small, short breaths and scanned the place for a paper bag.

"Do you know what you want?"

"Uh, yes. I like this script, with maybe some color accents. Do you have any sort of topical numbing agent?"

VIEW FROM THE LAUNDRY CHUTE

He looked at me like I had three and a half heads. There is no topical numbing agent. I agreed to a font he suggested.

He told me to scoot my skirt down and sit on a little round stool with rollers, then lean forward with my elbows on my knees.

Try this at home. Find a little stool that scoots around on rollers, on a hard-wood floor. Sit on it and lean forward in the above-mentioned fashion and see how stable you are after, say, fifteen minutes.

"Wouldn't it be better if I lay down?" I asked quietly.

"Are you sure you're ready for this?" he asked, with what I took as impatience. I assured him that I was, even though I wasn't.

The sound is not unlike a weed-whacker, a sewing machine, or an electric steak knife.

My daughter asked if I was all right. My leg vibrated like a hummingbird's wing. He started. I didn't twitch away. It didn't feel good, but it wasn't that bad either. Kristin told me to say something. I couldn't. She took my picture. He gave me breathing intervals to regroup during the process. I clutched a table in front of me. He told me to put my arms back on my knees. His name was Chris Howell. He wrote the words I wanted beautifully across my back. It took him twenty minutes. He was gentle. He was certainly *careful*. We will be wedded in this words-on-skin way for the rest of our lives. That's when I noticed how truly exceptional his tattoos were.

He actually gave me a little smile. I was ashamed at my first impression. I chalked a little of it up to fear, and the rest to ignorance.

Throughout the evening I was asked to show people my tattoo.

"It's for when she's in the nursing home," my daughter explained.

It's better for her to think of these words in that way, because that is how they *are* meant. To the future nurse's aide, don't judge me, or think that I'd had no life aside from being an old woman in a nursing home. Remember that I'm not just a body.

And above all, *be careful with me.*

L.W.P.

DISCLAIMER:

This is my idea. It is solely my idea and it is splendid. Should this idea be implemented by other than me, it will be deemed stolen, plagiarized, or ripped off. Just because I may not have the fortitude and wherewithal to actually *implement* this marvelous idea, does *not* mean I should not have the rights to it. Indeed, should anyone actually *do* this, I should receive royalties, no less than fifty percent, and control over all creative decisions should someone proceed with MY idea, in lieu of me suing their pants off.

I have had a fascination with Lot's wife for as long as I can remember. I think it started in bible school around the same time I was accused of sticking my fingers into our pretty blond teacher's eyes when we all snuck up behind her and put our little hands over her baby blues while squealing "Guess Who??!!" Apparently, some child was a little too exuberant and jammed a tiny finger into said teacher's eye. She spun around and grabbed MY arm and made me sit in a corner. No Christian forgiveness HERE. I was mortified. I refused to make a plaster cast of my hand that day just to teach her a lesson. It may have been in this class that I first heard about Lot's wife. It might be the reason I became a feminist. Oh! *The injustice!*

He didn't even give her a name for Gods' sake!

Lot was a guy that lived in Sodom and Gomorrah. I guess it was a little like Minneapolis/St. Paul, the sister cities. Only Sodom and Gomorrah were more like Las Vegas, but even *worse*. God found out about all the bad stuff going on there, not like in Vegas where what you do stays there. So a couple of major angel guys were dispatched to Lot's house to ask him what the heck was going on. Lot had them in for dinner to discuss the whole mess. A bunch of angry men, much like the mob in *Frankenstein*, wanted to kill the angels. (I thought angels were immortal?) So, get this, Lot steps out on his porch and offers the mob his two virgin daughters to do with what they wanted if they would just go away and leave him and the angels alone. Nice guy, huh? But the angels intervened and turned the mob blind so they would go away, albeit in a rather clumsy fashion.

It gets even worse. So on behalf of God, the angels tell Lot he better gather his wife and daughters and get the hell out of town. Most importantly they were NOT to look back. First thing in the morning, after breakfast, they took off. Probably Lot's wife and daughters did all the dishes from the party the night before as well as all the packing. They leave, and as they get to the top of the hill, Lot's wife suddenly realizes she may have left the iron on, or forgot the kids' precious plaster hand casts from bible school, so she turns around and POOF! She gets turned into a pillar of salt. Now she's a giant salt lick for the cattle and water buffalo of the region.

The rest of the family keep moving like nothing had happened. Lot settles himself and his two daughters in a cave and proceeds to have sex with them, then blames *them* for giving him too much wine! Lot was a pedophile and an incestuous pimp. I'm thinking the WRONG person stood in a field somewhere being licked by a cow.

And this is why I've been thinking about opening up a little place, a place where people can hang around comfortably and discuss philosophy, politics, domestic issues and art while enjoying cocktails and really salty snacks.

Lot's Wife's Place is that place. It would be my way to honor her while making some money too.

This is my vision. Lot's Wife's Place, or L.W.P., as hipsters would call it, would be a bistro in a chic little town *or* a neat section of a big city, like Little Five Points in Atlanta, or the DUMBO area of Brooklyn (Down Under the Manhattan Bridge Overpass).

The interior would be black and white, with huge black and white tiles on the floor and Ansel Adam-ish panorama photos of the Bonneville Salt Flats on the walls. The tables would be reminiscent of the kind we see in Marx Brothers Movies. They would have floor-length white linen tablecloths and little deco lamps in the center. There would be crystal salt dips on the tables as well, filled with the finest kosher salt from the Dead Sea. I would have seating areas here and there with comfortable, over-stuffed loveseats. These areas would be set off by diaphanous white material hung from ceiling tracks. Tiny hidden fans would cause the material to billow ever so slightly. Are you with me so far?

Here's my favorite part. The bathrooms would have nameplates that read "Sodom" and "Gomorrah." Sodom would be the men's room, naturally. The wait staff would wear white peg pants and white Nehru jackets topped off with white fez hats. This would give them a kind of "pillar" appearance. The cocktail menu would feature things like Salty Dogs and Margaritas. For lunch we'd offer salt pork sandwiches. There would be bowls of saltwater taffy along the polished wood bar. I'd have a salt boutique with rare salts from around the world. As you leave you would see a sign above the door that said, Thank You For Coming. Don't Look Back.

Perhaps I'd even have a Name Lot's Wife contest for the grand opening. She deserves no less.

Years ago, I sent this whole prospectus to Robert Fulghum, an author who actually mentioned Lot's wife in one of his books, *All I Really Need to Know I Learned in Kindergarten*. I took it as a sign that my idea would, in fact, be an excellent one because other people have thought about her as well.

I received a letter from him saying that I should let him know when L.W.P. opens because he looked forward to visiting and ordering a Margarita with "lots and lots of salt."

ON BEING FAT

Fat is cumulative like snow, algebra, and dust bunnies.

It creeps in and settles so comfortably that you don't even notice it at first. There are little hints here and there, like underwear feeling a little tight and leaving red seam marks on your waist for days, or shirts becoming clingy. You can blame these things on the dryer, or the quality of the fabric. But when the men's pants you bought (because you liked the baggy look) become pants that no longer zip, you realize that there is nothing to blame but the chips.

When you first notice your fat in a real and meaningful way, tears are shed. They fall when you see pictures of yourself on Facebook and your reflection in stuffy dressing room mirrors with bad lighting. There are tears when you can no longer see your toes, or that cool navel ring which has disappeared into a sinkhole of fat, never to be seen again. You just had to leave it down there.

When I first noticed I was fat, I ran from cameras, or stood strategically behind people in group pictures, resting my head on someone's shoulder. I wouldn't allow the nurse to tell me my weight when I went to the doctor. It was as if she was going to tell me how many days I had to live. I avoided mirrors and shiny things as much as possible. I bought maternity clothes. I walked as if I was bowlegged because I didn't want to feel my thighs touching. I also noticed, in the few pictures I permitted, that I stood with my arms away from my body like a body-builder who can't put his arms down against his sides. My breasts had expanded, creeping around to my back by way of my armpits to meet-up with the back boobs that were forming, similar to an inner tube pushed up under my arms.

I decided to give in. I changed my profile on a dating site to "a few extra pounds" and no longer gave a rat's ass how many chins I had. (Gee! I only have TWO so far . . .)

The very idea of admitting out loud that I am fat is a liberating experience. My name is Debbie, and I am fat. I will tell anyone who'll listen how much I weigh. It's like talking about a difficult childbirth. I brag that soon the airlines will charge me for TWO seats. I joke that in another month the fire department will have to cut me out of my bedroom and haul me off to a rehab facility. I anticipate the swell diet pills I'll be able to get LEGITIMATELY. Now I buy big caftans in loud colors; instead of only black ones. What the hell? I'm even pleased with pictures that reveal only ONE of my extra wattles. To me, that's a great shot.

I've become fairly complacent with my corpulence. I'm no longer consumed with despair 24/7, just 24/3. Speaking of

VIEW FROM THE LAUNDRY CHUTE

consuming, maybe I'll get a pizza with anchovies tonight . . . gluten free.

THE THEATER

Please God, deliver me from plays that involve body parts.

My sister insisted we go see *Menopause the Musical*. She bought tickets up front before polling to find out how many of us would actually go. The theater is not cheap. I don't mean the movie-type theater which is horrid at twelve-plus dollars a ticket, plus twenty-seven fifty for popcorn and water, not including tax. She bought tickets for *live* theater.

I love the theater, don't get me wrong, but you can get tickets for a show in New York cheaper than Tampa. In New York you only stand in line for twenty minutes in Times Square, at a certain time of day. You name the show you want and get a ticket for, like, twenty bucks. Most of the theaters are small, so even the seats way in back aren't too terrible, unless you suffer from vertigo or oxygen deprivation, or still wear stillettos.

Needless to say, we wouldn't have saved money by boarding a plane to New York to buy tickets. Can you envision it? A plane full of

VIEW FROM THE LAUNDRY CHUTE

pre, post, and peri-menopausal women crammed into two rows for the express purpose of flying to New York to save ten bucks a ticket to see a play about bodily functions?

Beloved sis was bursting with joy because she bought ten tickets, for which she wasn't even sure she'd have takers, just to see a musical about a malady that's about as pleasant as constipation. She had faith that there would be nine other women who would want to see that. How could I say no? She even requested I round up a few of my friends. I found one who would go. Nancy is game for anything, and, like me, has a hard time saying no, which is precisely why I asked her. I invited other friends via e-mail because I didn't have the ovaries to ask them face-to-face. *They* didn't have a problem with the N-word.

Miraculously, the tickets were dispersed and my sister did not have to re-mortgage her house. The show was amusing, but it wasn't really the genre I care to see. My taste lies more along the lines of *Waiting for Godot*. The women were funny and could sing and dance pretty well. The play was packed with popular songs that were cannibalized and re-worked to showcase subjects like hot flashes, night sweats, weight gain, and insanity. My row of 10 laughed until they cried. It was a fun evening all in all because they sold wine there.

But this doesn't end with musicals about menopause. A friend called and asked if I wanted to go see the *Vagina Monologues*. I told her my vagina has its own monologue, "When are ya gonna sweep the dust outta here and invite someone in?" But again, NO is an almost imperceptible word for me. So there we were, four women in a jeep driving through torrential rain and hail, bound for St. Pete on a Sunday evening to listen to a woman recount everything vaginal. When we finally arrived, soaking wet, we were told that it was sold out. Apparently there are many people who are interested in vaginal angst. We were bereft and alone with our shattered dreams, not to mention our vaginas. My brother lives nearby. Again, wine saved the evening.

I think someone ought to put together a one-man show called *The Penis Platitudes.* Can you imagine two hours of a guy going on and on about his one-eyed monster from puberty to prolapse? What about a musical? Someone could put together a song and dance extravaganza entitled *Great Balls o' Fire!* Dancing sperm would be cool, but Woody Allen has already done that.

A documentary would be awesome. *The Other Brain*, a retrospective of lies, deceit, and reckless behavior spawned in an area of the body far removed from the average male's actual cerebellum that overrides and inhibits rational thought processes. This documentary would pose provocative questions like, are wars organ related? Is size commensurate with car choices? Do presidents make decisions based on signals from this "second brain?" Maybe we could get someone like Hugh Hefner to produce it, but someone who is still alive.

I might actually be interested in penis productions. At least it would be a subject I'm not terribly familiar with. After all, I pretty

VIEW FROM THE LAUNDRY CHUTE

much know almost everything I care to know about menopause and my vagina and I'm OK with that.

Is it hot in here, or is it me?

BICYCLES

Riding a bicycle is bad for you. You could get your bell bottoms stuck in the spokes and get your leg ripped off. You could get hit by a garbage truck or a Volkswagen. A low-hanging branch could decapitate you. You might hit a squirrel and have his death on your head for the rest of your life. You could lose your virginity on the sissy bar. Why do they call it a sissy bar if it steals everyone's virginity? They should call it a slut-dog bar. Your front wheel could dive into an open manhole thrusting you headfirst onto the pavement and pushing your head down between your shoulders so you look like a football player forever. Guys will expect you to spit and pat their asses. The tires could blow because some stupid kid's stupid pencil box popped open when he dropped his stupid backpack, spilling stupid tacks everywhere. You could be going seventy-six miles an hour, hit the tacks, and die. The brakes could be too sensitive and . . . never mind. OR you could be like me and stay in bed where it's safe and snug and you never have to worry about getting hurt, just cruise along on the clouds, dreaming wonderful dreams.

Until a sinkhole opens up right under your house.

ANOTHER THOUGHT

I really don't mean to brag, but my life is what it is and that's just a fact. I managed to sleep until 2:30 today and the dreams were pure genius, even if I can't remember them entirely. In one dream a friend crashed a wedding where there were thousands of people all dancing in sync. She ran into the crowd from a meadow dressed as a mosquito and immediately lunged at people, attaching herself to them, one by one, to suck their blood.

In another dream I was gorgeous and was sitting with three other gorgeous women in a restaurant in Miami. A bunch of Spanish women stared at us through the window with looks of horror on their faces. "Why," one of my friends realized, "they think we're GHOSTS!"

Dreams are not required to make sense.

When I put my mind to it, I can go right back to sleep to continue my dreams.

But when it comes to getting things done in the here and now, my plans usually fail to materialize. I plan to update three calendars for the new year. Then, if time allows, I plan to shave the calluses off the bottom of my feet. Anatomy is SO amazing how it adapts, don't you think? Before the day is done, I also plan to drag the hose around the house for an hour and water plants. No fancy sprinkler system for *this* girl!

I have some apology notes to write to people based on behavior at a recent party that I don't really want to go into. When I'm done with those, I should iron some clothes because the stack is as tall as the Tower of Babel. I will reward myself with a nap if I accomplish these things. In my nap-dream all of my chores will be done or irrelevant and I can go back to scaring Spanish ladies through a restaurant window.

PICA DI UH-OH

Kiaralinda is a foodie. I learned the word foodie on HGTV cooking shows, but she does not consider herself knowledgeable about food. See, she would tell you she's an artist (she is), a traveler (she is), and a collector of interesting people (she is), but not a foodie.

She's also a pretty good cook. She picks up tips here and there and incorporates her experiences into food that's pretty darned great. She does this with her art, but you can't eat her art. Well, you could if you were Buster, my friend Sylvia's cocker spaniel.

I only know what I've eaten at their house (Todd lives there, too), or on their boat. I don't recall spitting anything out. To me, this is indicative of a good cook. The point is, I was happy when she called to invite me to dinner. I'd been working overtime and things had been a little stressful, so we hadn't had a chance to watch this season of *Project Runway* together like we do every fall when she and Todd are home.

I'd just brought in groceries, which included an awesome mojo-flavored roasted chicken. I had planned to carve off a slab for dinner and read an essay about a guy who spent time among the fans of Manchester United, a soccer team. These guys seem to be slightly more evolved than mammals from the Paleolithic age. I think that's an overly-generous assessment. The writer had "embedded" himself among these thugs. It's fascinating to read about disgusting people.

Kiaralinda had been working on a dish called picadillo, which she'd made with turkey. She asked if I'd like to join them for dinner, and then watch PR? Good food and fashion design seemed like a better option than a slab of chicken with a side of violence. I said I'd be over as soon as I put the groceries away. The phone rang again. Did I like raisins? No, but I told her that I'd pick them out. She told me it's difficult to pick them out because the picadillo would be wrapped in lettuce. I told her not to worry about it. She insisted that it would be no problem to make some on the side without raisins. I grabbed what was left of a bottle of Gato Negro and walked across the street.

The kitchen smelled great. Fresh green beans were steaming next to a pan of really good-looking rice stuff. Three colorful ceramic plates were lined up on the mosaic-tiled counter. The colors of the plates blended with the tiles. To the untrained eye, there weren't any plates. Along the counter there are always important business cards, pictures, phone numbers, and calendar dates. Space for plating is at a minimum. These people have busy lives.

VIEW FROM THE LAUNDRY CHUTE

Kiaralinda dished out the picadillo, deciding to use the lettuce as a garnish. Carefully, she laid the freshly steamed green beans around the rice on each plate. My raison-less plate was in the middle. I asked if she had any salt. I am totally crass when it comes to salt and pungent spices. Years of smoking and indulging in other unmentionable things have pretty much killed a refined sense of taste and smell for me. She brought a container of sea salt out of the cupboard. Without even tasting the food, I proceeded to shake salt on my plate. It wasn't coming out. I adjusted the holes. It still didn't come out. At this point I employed the heel-of-hand-to-bottom-of-container method. The top (which was at the bottom) flew off and an avalanche of sea salt cascaded over my food and the plate to my left. Todd, in his typically understated manner, asked, "Did you get enough salt?"

I was mortified. I tried to eat my food anyway saying, "SEE, it's not that bad! I can eat it! It will be OK! I'll just push the salt off to the side!" I felt as though I would throw up. It was nastier than that stuff you have to drink before a colonoscopy. But even WORSE, I had ruined someone *else's* plate of food. Everything within a foot of it was covered with salt. It was horrible. Kiaralinda stoically announced that there was plenty on the unspoiled plate to divide among us. What a trooper! She proceeded to divide one plate of food on to two more. I didn't realize that as she was doing this, she was meticulously trying to pick out raisins. Somehow, she lost grip of the plate and dumped all the rest of the picadillo on her shoes. It even looked good heaped on a sneaker.

I suggested we have roasted mojo chicken. It was close at hand, and barely cold in my fridge. She still had a couple of unspoiled lettuce leaves and green beans.

RECIPE:

- One roasted chicken cut into slices.
- Lettuce, on which to arrange the slices.
- Steamed green beans.
- Some good cheap wine.
- *Project Runway* on DVDs.

No mention was made of my boorish behavior, which made for a superb dining experience.

This recipe will not work if you try to substitute *real* friends with artificial ones.

Solamente pollo y amor.

LINGO IN CUBESVILLE

I tore myself away from *Brave New World* to write this. I've never read it before, I'm ashamed to admit. Thing is, the book was written in the thirties and is still relevant today. I realized that it parallels my life in some ways, so I just had to write about it.

I care about words and I care about the creative use of words. In *Brave New World*, Huxley tells a story about people who are conditioned to *not* set themselves apart from everyone else. The same phrases, recorded and repeated under the pillows of young children two hundred times a night, were the phrases they repeated mindlessly in their adult lives for any given circumstance. It was all for the good of the "community."

We do that now. Well, *I* don't. But I'm a square peg at my job. I am talking specifically about office lingo. I come close to screaming out loud whenever I hear certain phrases. The one I hate the most these days is *reach out*.

This is a term that, when used, proves you know how to play the game. You're part of the team. You know the rules and are willing to abide by them for the greater good of the company. YOU are appropriate. YOU know the score and intend to climb that ladder above the minions.

Cubicle people say "reach out" constantly. They don't say, "I will call, email, text, IM, or talk to John Doe." They say, "I will reach out to John Doe." If John Doe gives them a hard time, they don't argue, debate, have a lively discussion, or tell him to ***k off. They say, "I spoke to John Doe and *pushed back* about the fact that he hasn't paid us. I will *reach out* to him again tomorrow."

I could go on and on about other terms that are waved around like signs that say, I'M ONE OF YOU. I BELONG HERE. But I want to propose a solution I've come up with to make the company workspace a tad more creative and esoteric. These phrases can be mixed and matched at will. There are many excellent old sayings just waiting to be dusted off and resurrected. They're so much more colorful than *drill down, on a granular level, push back*, and *reach out*.

I propose the following vernacular for the workplace:

1. Come what may.
2. Till the cows come home.
3. Does a bear poo in the woods? (Shit is not appropriate in the workplace.)
4. Sometimes you get the gold mine, sometimes you get the shaft.

5. Far out!
6. Don't worry, be happy. (Instead of *no worries*, another oft-used phrase.)
7. You can't teach an old dog new tricks.
8. Dodged a bullet.
9. Broke the ice.
10. Cat got your tongue?
11. Get the bugs out. (Instead of *scrub the statistics*.)
12. Poo or get off the pot. (See number three.)
13. He was fired. (Normally, you hear nothing. There's just an empty desk that everyone cannibalizes when they realize John Doe is not coming back.)

I shall now demonstrate the possible uses for some of these:

When will you meet your productivity?

Come what may!

Great, but how long can you continue to turn these accounts in late?

Till the cows come home!

Seriously. Did you get that list done that I gave you yesterday?

Does a bear poo in the woods?

John Doe said <u>he</u> did most of the work on those accounts.

Sometimes you get the gold mine, sometimes you get the shaft! This replaces *he threw me under the bus.*

We're going to go ahead and give you a 2% raise because you've done such an excellent job this year.

Far out!

You get the idea, right?

There's another expression these days that makes me want to poke my eye with a fork. I say, "Well, at least it's Friday and I can sleep in tomorrow." And the person to whom I'm talking says, "*Right?*" or "*I know! Right?*" In fact, they answer every statement of fact with, "*Right?*" or "*I know! Right?*"

I sound like a cranky person. That's because I am. You see, I'm twice as old as most of my coworkers. I feel like I work in a daycare sometimes. They remind me of the scarecrow in *The Wizard of Oz.* They have a piece of paper so they immediately feel smarter.

VIEW FROM THE LAUNDRY CHUTE

Conversely, years of life experiences and tough decisions only makes you one thing. Obsolete.

Maybe I should try harder to fit in. I will incorporate office jargon into my sentences. I will say, "I plan to *reach out* to Fung Wa's for lunch today. Would anyone like to *be on the same page?*"

MAILING ERNIE

Monday I came home to a rusted tricycle, a paper bag full of empty cigar boxes, a large, moldy garage mat, and a full bottle of white zinfandel. They were piled by my door like dead animals the cat brought home.

I knew Ernie was at it again.

Ernie is one of those rare individuals that warrants his own sitcom, or, at the very least, a human-interest story on PBS. You may know the "Ernie types." They are the characters among us who inspire long, speculative conversations. These folks are the source of funny stories. They are the people you cannot ignore, nor would you want to. They are the people that keep life colorful.

I met Ernie years ago when I took a job in a factory—a print shop, to be precise. It was a big, loud, dirty place. I'd never worked in this kind of an environment. Mind you, I'm no princess. I never worry about my nails, or getting dirt under them. I've pounded bottoms into hassocks with a rubber mallet, and pumped gas in a blizzard at the height of the shortage in the seventies. I've had numerous waitress jobs, managed a blue jean store, written a little column for a town paper, and sold concrete, cosmetics, and rain lamps. I have driven to hospitals thirty miles apart to review medical charts for Medicare. But in all of these scenarios, I had never met anyone quite like Ernie.

I took the job at the print shop for the benefits. It was supposed to be temporary until my massage practice could become more lucrative, I ended up working in the factory for nine years.

Anyway, Ernie had worked in print shops all his life. He knew how to operate a multitude of machines from stitchers to folders, and all of the strange apparatus in between. I always suspected that new hires were placed with Ernie as helpers to initiate them into the reality of the print shop.

Ernie was a big, lumbering guy from Newark, New Jersey. He had thick, silver hair that he combed into a DA (Duck's Ass) in the same manner as the Fonz or the guy in *Grease*. While we'd work, he'd tell a million stories, and some of them were probably true. He liked to quote *The Godfather*. His favorite line was "Vengeance is best when it's served cold." That was also his philosophy. He called me "kid." I liked being his helper. I could hold my own and I knew it wouldn't be a boring day. In short, we liked each other.

After he was fired, things began to appear on my porch. I moved twice, but the intermittent offerings would still find their way to my door. It was Ernie's way to make sure you wouldn't forget him, as if anyone ever could. I knew the stuff came from him because many of the stories he told me involved clandestine "drops" at the homes of friends, as well as enemies. There were no horse heads that I'm aware of, but for years I'd come home to find old toys, boxes of rubber bands, a wine rack, rolls of shrink wrap, two vintage Royal sewing machines, old beach chairs, t-shirts on wire hangers, shoes, and the contents of drawers, or perhaps glove compartments, consisting of expired AARP cards, broken pencils, drink coupons from Casino Cruises, doctors appointment cards, and movie ticket stubs.

Enough was enough. I had to get even. A few of my friends, who are artists by profession, provided the inspiration. They told me about a "mail art" gallery show they'd attended in Chicago. Mail art consists of things that creative people send to each other in the mail. Some were artistically embellished postcards and letters, but much of it was outrageous items that was decorated in some fashion, taken to the post office, and mailed *as is*. Believe it or not, you can mail just about anything.

The post office weighs the item, slaps a label on it, and off it goes. Sometimes it gets to the destination intact, sometimes not. But it doesn't matter.

The point is, whatever it was, it was delivered. That was the fun of it. People never knew what they would find in their mailboxes, or when. God forbid a lucky recipient would actually have to go to the post office and pick it up. Certain things can be embarrassing to lay claim to. The gallery show displayed examples of great things that made the journey, bowling balls included.

VIEW FROM THE LAUNDRY CHUTE

It occurred to me that I could do this to Ernie. I started to save the things he left on my porch. Then I turned them into something else and mailed them back. I wove rubber bands into an alligator postcard. An old eyeglass case was doused with the anisette liquor that had been left with it on my porch the day before. It became a holder for an original little story, with a picture on the other side. I made collages out of Ocean Spray labels from the empty bottles Ernie would leave combined with other things I'd find in the bags with them.

He started to leave bigger things to challenge me. I'd find a way to turn them into something and mail them back. Eventually, the porch offerings began to taper off. But I knew I hadn't won by a long shot. Ernie loved this shit.

It was during this time, probably inspired by Ernie and the Chicago gallery show, that a few of us began sending mail art to each other. I received collaged plastic bottles, 45 RPM records with designs painted on them, and once, a plastic martini glass, which didn't make it intact. (The postal people were kind enough to put the pieces in a Ziploc and deliver them.) I received Pez dispensers and plastic fish. Not to be outdone, I mailed a stuffed bra mounted on a board (like a dead fish) that was embellished with Hershey's kisses. I stood in line with it at the post office at Christmas time. Mothers shielded their children from me. Dunedin postal workers were very helpful and have excellent senses of humor, as do the Safety Harbor postal people, where the bra ultimately landed and had to be picked up by the recipient. The Hershey's kisses were no longer on it, just tattered pieces of silver foil. I learned that a discarded stiletto costs $2.88 to mail, and postage labels fit quite nicely across the toe.

Then Ernie delivered a beat-up straw hat which he propped against my back door.

I decided it was time to enlist the troops and do a "pass-the-hat" mail attack on him. I painted the hat lavender and wrapped it with a gold lamé band. I took it to the post office. I sent it to one of my co-conspirators with an attached list of names inside. Each recipient was to embellish it in some way, then mail it to the next person on the list. The hat passed through several hands. About a year later it was returned to the last person on the list, Ernie. Last, but certainly not least.

Ernie never made mention of the hat but sent a brief, scrawled note on the back of an old motor lodge post-card. The note stated he was going to Texas for the holidays to visit his kids. Life went on, the holidays came and went, and I moved again.

One Monday I came home to a rusted tricycle, a paper bag full of empty cigar boxes, a large crumpled roll of Tyvec, and a full bottle of zinfandel. Ernie had gotten me again. There, next to the wine, was the lavender embellished hat, with photos of it in every room of his house.

FEAR OF FLINGING

I realized I had a problem when I hung up a brand new, black shirt and discovered I already had two that were exactly like it. I do like black shirts. Specifically, I like scoop-necked, short-sleeved t-shirts in a cotton/spandex blend. But somehow I forgot that I already had one (or more), when I bought it.

I also tend to forget that I already have Duke's mayonnaise (three jars at last count) and black yoga pants (two pairs, still with tags) as well. God, I love yoga pants. No, I don't practice yoga. I practice eating macaroni salad made with Duke's mayo and the yoga pants allow me to do this comfortably. Still, when I pull my drawer out to put away my new black yoga pants, the exact pair stares back at me. It's delightful, like Christmas, but also disturbing, like being overdrawn at the bank.

I hope I'm not getting dementia. I remember going to my parents' house and discovering that the pantry was full of Bush's baked beans and little else. This was about the same time mail-ordered items from Mom were arriving at my door on a regular basis. I got things like Siamese cat salt and pepper shakers, several pairs, and ankle bracelets with bells on them like belly dancers wear.

I decided to Google obsessions and dementia. I hoped that my multiple purchases were merely an obsession. Obsessions are a little classier. I can at least tell people I've got obsessive compulsive disorder and take a drug for it. But dementia is not cool at all. It can involve adding Depends to the black shirt and yoga pant purchases.

According to the *American Heritage Dictionary*, an obsession is a compulsive preoccupation with a fixed idea, or an unwanted feeling or emotion. Psychiatrists have even categorized them:

1. Somatic obsessions (hypochondria, dysmorphophobia)
2. Physical obsessions (eating disorders like anorexia and bulimia)
3. Sexual obsessions (paraphilia), and pathological jealousy.

There does not appear to be a black shirt or mayonnaise obsession, although I did not specifically search psychosis/black shirt or psychosis/mayonnaise.

However, when I looked up senility, I found this definition:

A deterioration of intellectual faculties, such as memory, concentration, or judgment.

VIEW FROM THE LAUNDRY CHUTE

Judgment and memory. It appears I fit more into the senility category than the obsession category. Greaaaat.

I suppose this explains how I forgot how to open my car on the passenger side from the inside of the car. I pressed the unlock function on my key and the little button wouldn't go up. So I tried to grasp the little button and pull it up, but it was flush with the door panel so I couldn't get hold of it. I thought about trying tweezers, but I had no tweezers handy. I had a corkscrew, a pen, and a Swiffer Duster. I also had a front seat full of groceries. So, cursing under my breath, I dragged everything over the gearshift and schlepped the stuff around the front of the car to take it into the house. I then tried to unlock the passenger side from the outside with my key but the little button STILL wouldn't go up. So I dragged the rest of the stuff over the gear shift as well.

I told this story to a friend at work, lamenting that I'd have to get the lock fixed because otherwise I'd have to unload things across the driver's side, and passengers would have to climb in that way too.

"Why didn't you just open the passenger door with the door handle?" she asked.

"What do you mean?"

She looked alarmed. "The DOOR handle. Did you pull the handle?"

"Oh yaaaaaaa . . ."

I had flashbacks of my mom trying to turn on the TV with the phone, or clapping to turn off a lamp at my cousin's house, over and over again, while we wondered what the hell she was clapping about. I imagined myself in a facility flinging poo at the nurse's assistant.

Someone once said we become what we fear. Based on that premise, I will become a senile, fat spider in a filthy nursing home that serves only pureed food. I will have to exercise all the time and also climb sheer, high, rock mountains (when not scuba diving), then do lots of mathematical equations.

But I think I've wandered off-topic.

I work in an office that sends appeals to insurance companies. Lori, who I always call Shelly, used to work at United. She writes appeals to United now. I'm very familiar with her history at that insurance company. She asked me one day if I knew anyone there.

"Actually, I do. My cousin was an attendant and her husband was a big-wig there too, I think."

"Wow! How long were they with United? I might know them because I used to travel to the different offices."

"They both retired, so they must have worked there a long time. I don't know exactly when they retired. They live in a house on the west coast."

"Can you write their names down? I have a friend who's been in corporate for over thirty years. It would be cool if they knew each other."

I wrote down my cousin's name and told her they lived near San Francisco. I said I thought her husband had actually been a pilot with them.

VIEW FROM THE LAUNDRY CHUTE

She looked at me funny. "So he has his own plane?"

"No. He flew for the company."

"So he was a big-wig in corporate and he also flew the corporate plane?"

"No silly. He flew for everyone!"

Silence. That's when it occurred to me. I was talking about the airlines and she was talking about the insurance company. We had a good laugh over the silliness of it all. As soon as she went back to her desk, I downed six gingko biloba vitamins and brewed a cup of ginseng tea. I wondered if a person could OD on gingko.

Even though I'm fairly concerned about my mental faculties, I've decided to chalk it up to stress. When it can't be explained, blame it on stress. And besides, you really can't have too many yoga pants. They fade quickly, lose their cling, and get all snagged and stuff. I was just being smart buying extra ones. As for the mayonnaise, it can be used for soooooo many things. Imagine a home without mayo! Tuna just wouldn't hold the same fascination as it does with good mayonnaise, some onions, and green olives, six jars at last count.

Now why can't I get this damned TV to turn on?

Oh shit.

REPETITION REPEATS ITSELF

The night before was just like the night before that, and the night before that, and the night before that. Nights line up like a funhouse hall of mirrors, diminishing to a pinpoint of oblivion.

My mausoleum of cherished monotony begins the moment I get home from work, fumble with keys, and open the kitchen door.

The black one will body-slam the door and bitch at me as if it were the very first time I've left her alone for the whole day. Her nagging is fervent. I will bitch back at her in her native Fursee, for which I am fluent. The one in the cheap faux ocelot coat will sit patiently, pigeon-toed paws on each side of his belly like little parentheses.

The creatures of the house will do the same things that they did the night before, and the night before that.

VIEW FROM THE LAUNDRY CHUTE

I will grab a plastic bag and head to the litter box. The black one will run ahead of me, stomach swinging side to side even though the momentum is forward. She is a study in impossible kinetics. She will get to the box before I do. She will climb in to pee. It takes her five minutes to tidy up. I will wait, leaning my head against the wall. There is a smudge there from previous leanings. Then she will balance on the rim of the box, all fours gripping the edge, to poop like a defecating tightrope walker. Once she is satisfied that she's gotten another one over on me, she will stroll past, the epitome of entitlement. Only then will I be permitted to clean the box . . . just like I did that morning.

I will make dinner. It will be one of four things.

It will be a blue cheese burger, pre-made patties from Publix—because to actually make the patties and smoosh blue cheese into them is too much to ask of a cubicle zombie at the end of the day. I will have the burger with no bread, but with sliced avocado and a slab of red onion. If it was a really bad day I will add a clump of hot horseradish for self-flagellation.

Alternatively, I will have Matzos with perfectly sliced little discs of Spanish green olives, centered on top of each, then skillfully drizzled with hot pepper oil and topped with perfect triangles of picante provolone cheese. These square little things will be my addiction after 50 seconds in the microwave. Or I might have salmon, sautéed in Hoisin sauce, garlic, and safflower oil. It will be nestled next to a salad of baby kale and butter lettuce, NOT iceberg lettuce.

Iceberg lettuce is worthless. One of the things I've learned in my isolation over the years is that you shouldn't give it to your tortoise, much less your own damned self.

Or I will have rotini pasta with margarine, or whatever the hell it REALLY is, skillfully drizzled with hot pepper oil. This is often the meal choice on an instant gratification night.

I will pour two fingers of Gato Negro, a delightfully cheap wine, into a clear glass. My Parisian friend Annick told me that wine MUST be served in a clear glass. Only morons use opaque or colored glasses. I have never confessed to her that I occasionally use Solo cups. Solo cups are the official vessel for any kind of wine if one is in someone's back yard and there are plastic table cloths.

At the kitchen table, I will read a book that I keep in a special wire holder, currently it is *The Bed Wetter* by Sarah Silverman. I don't know if I can call this book a novel. I'm pretty sure it doesn't have enough pages. I will place my food and first glass of wine on the placemat.

This is officially my sacred time. This is the moment I long for all day. I would rather sit at my table with a book, passable food, and a glass of purple than do anything else in the world. This is MY time. After I've eaten, I will enjoy a cigarette and some weed.

Several nights a week I might Facetime a dear friend who lives in Upstate New York. She is pretty much homebound. I prop my phone against the book. She will answer from her bed. We will lose video several times and wonder whose phone is at fault.

VIEW FROM THE LAUNDRY CHUTE

About the only time she goes out is when her husband takes her to doctor's appointments. She has several and I have a hard time keeping track of them. There is the shrink, the neurologist, the pulmonary specialist, and the cardiologist. She's waiting for her aortic aneurism to get to be a 5.8 something before they will do anything about it. It could burst at any time. It is currently only at 5.7 something. But the insurance won't pay unless it is exactly a certain size. It seems close enough to me to take the fucker out of there.

I will then carry her face outside in the waning light of dusk and maybe show her the plants in the yard, or lizards doin' the nasty. The neighbor might be skateboarding down my driveway. She will show me things like the twinkle lights hanging from her window or the place in her dresser where Ed keeps his old pictures. She'll show me the hiding place for her ear buds because Walter, their cat, pulls them out of her ears when she's listening to a book and eats them. I saw him do it once. He also grooms her head.

She and I used to hang after work at Dale's Beach Bar when I was 22 and she was 26. We were skinny and hot (and not from the heat). I wore a 30-inch gold chain around my bare waist which emerged from low-slung Levi's and travelled upwards toward a butter leather halter-top embellished with pheasant feathers. She had cheekbones for miles, a tiny waist, and an impressive ass. She had Annie Lennox hair.

Now she worries about how they will make ends meet since Orange Man (at this writing the current president) slashed Medicaid.

They get $600 less each month. They only qualify for $16 of food stamps, because with their combined Social Security checks they make 50 dollars too much. She's not sure she'll be able to keep doing Weight Watchers. At one point she lost almost twenty pounds. But Ed's been making her bagels in the morning, and homemade ice cream for the evenings.

Once we end the call, I will go to bed and watch *Law & Order* reruns until I fall asleep, only to awake the next day to go to work and begin looking forward to when it will be sacred time again in my mausoleum of cherished monotony.

It occurs to me that my friend has her own mausoleum, but it probably doesn't feel terribly sacred to her. After all, she did not choose her circumstances. She'd rather get out and visit people. But if she gets another night, that means she gets another day, just like the night and day before.

And I will carry her face around my yard again.

HOLD THE TOMATOES

We sat across the table from each other in a local eatery I like to frequent. A pierced and tatted, hip young man was ready to take our orders. The person with whom I was sharing dinner asked, "Are there any seeds, like poppy-seeds or peppercorns, in the burger or the bun? If you don't know, please find out. And please leave the strawberries off the summer salad. I have diverticulitis and you've no idea how painful it is."

I died a thousand little deaths as I watched him recount his disease, complete with hand gestures indicating where the colon is found in his body and how the seeds lodge (a jabbing motion with his finger), in the soft pink lining and then become inflamed (the same hand gesture commonly used for an explosion). He waited for a response from the server to assure him that he understood the gravity of the matter.

I blocked both of them out and slipped into a fantasy fog. In it I'm ordering in the same fashion.

"I'll take the kale salad because iceberg lettuce creates tumult in my stomach. You don't want me to crop dust my way outta here, believe me. Besides, there is absolutely no nutritive value in iceberg lettuce. I had a turtle that almost died from malnourishment because I fed him iceberg all the time. The vet said NO iceberg. And puleeeeze remove the tomatoes if there are any because they remind me of cat placenta, especially the stewed tomatoes which wouldn't be the kind used on a salad, but you know what I mean. Also, if you don't mind, please leave the raw beets off of the salad as well. They make me pee red and I always forget that I've eaten beets so I get scared that I might be hemorrhaging. And I'd like a vodka tonic. Oh wait . . . tonic makes me belch like a man. I'll have a pinot grigio. And would you be so kind as to bring a bunch of toothpicks? I have gaps in my teeth from receding gums and dry-mouth that I get from my meds. I can't smile at all after I eat because my teeth catch bits of food as efficiently as Phil Rizzuto caught grounders."

"Ma'am?"

I snapped out of it, realizing that our server and my dinner companion were staring at me as if I'd had a little stroke. I wiped the smirk off my face.

"I'll have the kale salad, hold the tomatoes. And would you please bring me a toothpick? Oh, and two pinot grigios?"

QUANTUM PHYSICS AND THAI FOOD

We went to a lecture at the University of South Florida about quantum physics. It was free, and three of my friends wished to go. All I had to do was ride along like a dog going to the park for a playdate. I refrained from sticking my head out of the window to let the breeze blow my ears back.

The four of us included David (my male girlfriend), Nancy, the smartest and most innocent person I know, and Bettina, an artist of photography from Hamburg who's as cute as a speckled pup under a red wagon. Her use of the English language is a puzzle to decipher. For example, she explained that she was seeking a job more suited to her abilities. She said, *I chust must sink around ze corner.* It took me awhile to realize that she meant she needed to think "outside of the box." She has always sported red hair cut in the style of a flapper from the twenties. She weighs about ninety-eight pounds fully clothed, in heavy wool, that's soaking wet.

David really has no clue about the quantum thing unless it involves James Bond in some way. He is a chemist though, so of the four of us probably knew the most. He's always game when it comes to hanging with us girls. His priority is texting. He does it constantly because of the online dating thing. He usually has a few irons in the fire. David belongs to Plenty of Fish in the Sea and one for a heavier group called Plenty of Whales. He also belongs to Desperately Seeking Anyone and Not Dead Yet. I'm making him sound like a player but he really isn't. He's genuinely trying to find the one person who will give him a forever home. Unfortunately, he has a little problem with the way he communicates. He'll say to his date, "I'll pick you up in 17 minutes and 37 seconds, maybe 18 minutes and 40 seconds." The prospective life-long companion is thinking, HUH? One hour later he arrives to pick her up.

Nancy has a voice you can distinguish in a crowd. If we could somehow track and record the voices of angels like we can whales, hers would be high and ethereal. She's an earth angel. She happened to be at the vet the same night I was there with my cat Lester. She'd brought a neighbor's dog in to get shots. That night she picked up my tab. She has helped everyone I know in some way. She's extraordinarily bright but does stupid things on occasions, like go to a bike race and ride the whole course before figuring out it was the wrong weekend (she wondered why there were no water stops along the route).

We arrived at the auditorium and sat in a row, David, Nancy, Bettina and I. We anticipated a lecture on positive thought and manifestation. The first speaker asked how many of us were graduate students. About three quarters of the people raised their hands. Then he asked how many specifically had masters or doctorates in physics. There were about half as many hands. Then he asked, "How many of you have never gone to college or taken any physics?" It was my hand that went up, only mine.

We listened to an hour of Holographic Physics at the Micro and Macro Level. We heard "extrapolations, and experiments that produced various statistics and the quantification of intention versus attention." We saw numerous graphs and charts. A woman in front of us nodded knowingly after everything the speaker said. Several people murmured in appreciation when specific studies were mentioned. David napped. Nancy listened intently. Bettina sucked on a 24 oz. bottle of water. She's very health-conscious. Trouble is, the water bottle made a loud collapsing sound when she drank from it. I'm sure there's a scientific explanation for the expanding and contracting of a plastic bottle when a vacuum is introduced. The woman in front of us, between copious note-taking, glanced back in our direction. I sank down in my seat having already identified myself as an imbecile.

David leaned over to me between naps. His cell phone had received a message. The vibration woke him up. He whispered that metaphysics preceded physics. Or maybe it's the other way around. I was just surprised that he was able to follow this shit even while napping.

Bettina decided it was time for a *helsee schnack*, so she passed three packs of wasabi peas down to us. These are crispy things in loud cellophane wrappers. There we were, the four of us, opening plastic bags that crackled every time we dipped into them. We crunched on the treats like hyenas on bones. The woman in front was twisting her neck to glare at us by this time. I was sure she was going to have a bad case of "whiplash-caused-by-ignorant-people." I am, after all, a massage therapist. I know these things.

It was time to ask questions. I wanted to know if the genius speaker had been a latchkey child. I wanted to know the difference between MICRO and MACRO when applied to stuff that's invisible anyway. I wanted to know how a device could be random, or if random was a type of device. I really, really wanted to know where the ladies room was located. I asked none of these questions, again, having already identified myself as an imbecile.

The *schnacks* were only a tease. We decided to skip out early. The lecture was obviously not of a metaphysical nature. There was no mention of crystals or positive thought processes. I decided to look up Metaphysics for Dummies on my phone while Bettina and Nancy argued whether the Thai restaurant was on Fletcher or Fowler.

VIEW FROM THE LAUNDRY CHUTE

Metaphysics, according to my phone, is the ability to alter the real world just by the power of positive or negative thought. We manifested Fletcher as the correct address for the restaurant. Sure enough, we found the place right where we thought it would be! But when manifesting, one must be very specific about details.

It was closed.

THE COOKOUT

The morning I woke up on the kitchen floor, I remembered something about a cheap bottle of wine and bad eggrolls. I find hard, cold terrazzo very comforting sometimes. My phone buzzed. It was my friend David asking if I wanted to go to a cookout. He said he had an invitation from a woman he'd met on the internet, Eunice. They were just friends. She thought it would be nice if he brought me along to a little party she was having. Nothing fancy, just some steaks on the grill.

My parents had the best cookouts. "Bar-b-cuing" was a *verb* which meant that we were going to throw hotdogs and burgers on the brick grill which was out on the patio behind the house. One of my favorite things about summer were those patio cookouts, the picnic table covered with a red and white checkered cloth, and whatever Mom added to make the table pretty. Relaxing summer evenings on the patio.

David said that Eunice shared his love of photography. Her camera was a Hasselblad. My friend Bettina was an excellent photographer and used that model also. So I was interested to meet Eunice. He said we were going to go to the beach to capture the sunset before the party. I decided that I was probably physically and emotionally able to ride in a car, watch the sun set, sit in a lounge chair, and eat a steak, even though I felt like hell. There was plenty of time to throw up, should the need arise, as well as cover the dark circles under my eyes with some wood putty before David picked me up at four.

On the way I suggested that we stop and get Eunice some flowers and a ring of cocktail shrimp. It is polite to do these things, I advised him. Sometimes he needs prodding on social graces.

We arrived at her "compound," a deed-restricted gated community complete with a guard. After we explained why we were there and gave him our social security numbers and birth certificates, he allowed us to proceed through the big, iron gate that had spikes on top.

Eunice had asked us to park by the pool which turned out to be approximately three city blocks from her door. I assumed we were asked to park there to accommodate the guests that were coming. She told David that there were only two guest spaces. It was not a walk I particularly cared to make because it was a ninety-degree, August afternoon and I was still not feeling awfully swell.

The door opened. A petite blonde shoved her hand at me and pumped my arm up and down as if she expected me to spew water from my mouth. I was surprised she wasn't bigger, rounder. Usually, David likes more substantial women. She turned her back on us and went about arranging a floor-full of camera equipment. We stood in the doorway, wondering how we'd maneuver around the artificial Christmas tree and the stuff on the floor.

I chalked the situation up to artistic eccentricity.

So we took it upon ourselves to weave around the stuff. As I stepped over expensive equipment I began to wish bad things on David because there was no evidence of an upcoming party in this place. I opened the back door in the utility room. No patio. We became part of the furniture as she fussed with the equipment, talking to herself while dashing in and out of rooms. David held the flowers, and I, the shrimp. We'd been standing in the middle of the room for an awkward amount of time when she finally remembered we were there and waved us over to the couch.

She was a darling little British thing but I was not feeling terribly fond of her. I handed her the shrimp. She asked what she was to do with the *PRAWNS*. I told her she was to EAT them. She asked how they should be cooked. I told her they were already cooked. She insisted they were raw because they were cold. I told her that we could safely eat them as they were but they needed to go in the fridge. She asked if she should make some sort of sauce or cook them in the oven with sausages. I explained that there was cocktail sauce *with* them. She looked at me suspiciously, as if I were pranking her. David handed her the flowers and she asked him what she was supposed to do with *them*. I concluded that her expertise was limited to photography.

VIEW FROM THE LAUNDRY CHUTE

We sat on the couch for nearly an hour. I was severely dehydrated. Eunice was very intent with her equipment. I suspected she was not going to offer us a drink any time soon and I didn't want to interrupt her creative process.

I found the bathroom. Once inside, I locked the door and turned the water on in the sink where I could just fit my head under the spigot to drink like a person who'd just dragged herself across Death Valley.

She instructed us to schlep tripods, wooden boards, and camera bags all the way back to David's car. It seemed like it was awfully late to be chasing sunsets, but I'm not a pro in these matters. I sat on the boards in the back seat of David's Volkswagen among fast-food wrappers and plastic Hello Kitty toys.

As we drove down U.S. 19 I attempted to engage Eunice in conversation. Leaning over her seat I told her that my daughter is a road manager for punk bands and had recently driven from Leeds to Glasgow. She sent me a postcard of colorful sheep on a misty hill. On the back of the card Kristin explained how the sheep, when in the fog, appeared to be a "tie-dyed hill" because their rumps were dyed all different bright colors and it made her laugh every time she saw them bounding across the hills with their blue, red, yellow, and pink butts bobbing up and down.

"Well, you *KONT* tie-dye a sheep. That's absurd!" Eunice said in the rearview mirror. "They must have been *BEAN* marked after they were tested for the *hoof and mouth*. Yes, I'm certain that must

118

have *BEAN* why they were marked. Of course, this would render the wool useless, so they must have *BEAN SHEDULED* to be killed."

We arrived at the beach just in time to watch the sun crash into the gulf. Now I hated David AND Eunice. Still, she wanted to haul the crap through the sand and set it up. Like obedient, healthy sheep, we did as we were told. She carried the camera.

Apparently, she knew *nothing* about that camera or any of the equipment because she asked David to set the stuff up. She asked him which buttons to press to take a picture. He asked if she had a light meter. Blank eyes. Blank eyes looked back at him. For another forty-five minutes he explained F-stops and apertures.

No one showed up for the cookout, which turned out to be two pieces of sausage broiled until black and the kitchen full of smoke. Eunice wasn't certain how to determine if the sausages were done. I assured her that when they catch on fire, they're done.

She'd also arranged some *LOOVLY GREENS* topped with chunks of cold, leftover steak that had congealed fat along the sides, and unpeeled orange halves. She said she saw on a cooking show that steak and oranges were good on *GREENS*. She decided to make *PO TOT OH* salad even though it was almost eight o'clock. She still had to boil the potatoes and everything. It was *then* that it occurred to her to offer us a drink. David was asleep on the couch. She opened a pack of Crystal Light and mixed up a batch. I drank the whole pitcher and mixed a second one myself.

VIEW FROM THE LAUNDRY CHUTE

She attempted to make conversation with me since David was asleep. She took me upstairs to see her cat. There on the bed was an adorable, fat orange tabby. I said, "OH! Aren't you a little fatty?"

"He's not FAT! He is merely big-boned!" She turned and ran down the stairs.

So much for bonding with the hostess. As I approached the couch, I whispered in David's ear. "*You're a dead man.*"

The table was set with three placemats, but no flowers because she put them on top of the washing machine in the utility room. There *were* napkins and utensils. David and I had bowls of what looked like compost, the *LOOVLY GREENS*. There was a plate in the middle of the table with two, small, charcoaled sausages.

Eunice finally tried a shrimp (*PRAWN*). (At least we still had those to eat.) She liked them so much she pulled the whole ring over to her placemat and ate the entire thing while we hacked at our black sausage and congealed steak with orange halves compost salad. The *PO TOT OHS* had not yet come to a boil.

There was no grill that night. No comfy lounge chairs. No guests. She couldn't understand why no one came or called or emailed. I was pretty sure I knew why. She was not just eccentric; she was *DAFT, MAD AS A HATTER*, and a fucking *LOONEY*. Did I mention she was an elementary school teacher?

David and I stopped for Chinese on the way home.

Hold the eggrolls.

IT'S THE JOURNEY

"It's not the destination, it's the journey."

I've read this quote so many times and always thought of it as a lame motivational cliché.

But as I've become older, I realize that there are some teeth to it. For what is life but hundreds and thousands of tiny journeys? Every time we awake from the respite of night we begin a new day trip. When we open our eyes, they may alight on something we've not noticed before. The angle of the sun on the wall and how it frames the picture hanging there, and something in that picture that eluded us before. Maybe there's a dusty cobweb we need to knock down. A new grey hair on the dog's snout.

Each day brings new conversations, new realizations, new decisions, new sounds, visuals, and smells. Or the same old, same old.

Each day brings a sense of well-being or a new pain along with a hope that the well-being lasts or the damned pain goes away. Our bodies can be relied upon to contribute new sensations with which to

VIEW FROM THE LAUNDRY CHUTE

deal as we commence our journey. Sometimes a back pillow will not be enough.

Maybe someone, on this day, will say something funny, or something that pisses us off. Something that uplifts, that educates, something that makes us feel loved, or something that makes us feel small and bitter.

Every day brings a new challenge or the same challenges, but more likely a combination of both. We feel anticipation, boredom, energy, lethargy. We are grateful, resentful, empathetic, indifferent, creative, pensive, articulate, amusing, or at a loss for words. Feelings are infinite and finite—it may be only one you have all day.

We may awaken and remain in bed, paralyzed. The damned ethereal bus idles just outside the bedroom door. We can remain here and make everyone who shares this journey today wait. Or we can get on with it. So the doors swing open and we climb in with passengers who will take this trip with us. Some fellow-travelers reek of darkness and anger. They smell of sweat and urine. Some are so cheerful you want to gag them, the Happy Kathys of the world, who never fail to say *good morning* and smell of soap and powder.

We take in sights as we ride. We pass mass murders from last week and vultures like finials on telephone poles. There are billboards extoling the virtues of having a job, no matter how crappy. Billboards that remind us how old we are. Have we planned ahead? Billboards extoling fabulous places to travel and billboards telling us we never will. We deal with whomever we sit next to that day. Our seatmates constantly change. One may chatter on and on about her accomplishments, about a Netflix binge she and her husband shared over the weekend. Almost everyone is in pairs, like Noah's Ark. But some of us know we will become extinct because we are dying alone, leaving nothing and no one for the future . . . maybe not on this trip, but surely on one of these buses someday.

It makes stops along the way. Some get off and catch another ride. We know we are going to the same place as yesterday and the day before. But sometimes a fellow traveler gets to choose. Sometimes the place we disembark is a horrible, painful place. Sometimes it is a place we try to visit again because it brought us joy, whatever that is. The driver ultimately decides.

The point is, I kind of understand that cliché now, because the destinations for each of us change all the time. They change every day. A goal comes and goes . . . is either realized or abandoned. A resolution is kept, or tossed out the window. A dream materializes or evaporates in the sun. The myriad of possibilities, different for everyone, with infinite variations.

Yet the ultimate destination is the same for us all.

So it occurred to me that the most important part of any journey is not *"when are we gonna get there?"* but what will unfold on this *one* day? There's no hurry. But damned if the bus seems to go faster and faster every week. Will any of the souvenirs we accumulated on one trip be packed to go on the next? Will we downsize and make room for new stuff? Will the overhead bins be

VIEW FROM THE LAUNDRY CHUTE

full and threaten to crash down upon our heads? Or will they be forever empty?

Each journey we take informs our spirit and becomes part of our DNA.

Take pictures along the way to burn another day.

ACKNOWLEDGEMENTS

Oy.

This is the part where I try to thank everyone who has helped me put this thing together. Let me tell you, it isn't easy. If I had known it would be hard work, I would have quit. I don't like to work hard unless someone pays me. To voluntarily pursue a passion, and then have to work at it is just ... I don't know, masochistic.

I am not a worldly person. I've never been out of the U.S., unless you count Canada. So my stories come from the day-to-day business of life. They exist because of a plethora of material provided by family, friends, and strangers with whom I come in contact. Without these people, who are and were in my life, I'd have had to be a fiction writer, and those people are fucking crazy.

The Safety Harbor Writers and Poets are friends (and a family that I chose). They helped me harness my thoughts and provided endless feedback and technical instruction over the years that have made this first little book possible. I have lots of stories, so maybe there will be a couple more books. Who knows?

These are the specific people from Writers Group who listened to these stories over and over and found the most bizarre shit that I never would have noticed. Thank you to Warren Firschein, Laura Kepner, Carrie Granato, Barbara Finkelstein, N.B., Christopher Shaun, Amy Bryant, and Nicole Caron. There have been many creative individuals who have circulated through the group and who are currently members. I thank them as well for bringing things to light.

Posthumous thanks go out to Romeo Lemay, a very elegant, and sometimes naughty, gentlemen who wrote gorgeous stories about growing up in Canada. He was well-known here in Safety Harbor because he was out and about in his scooter, always a bag of dog biscuits in the basket. He was the oldest member of the S.H.W. & P.

Then along came Dr. Roger Howard. We only had him for a short while, but his poetry blew me away. He was game for antics, and we shared a love of the works of Billy Collins. I have several of his books. I believe, had he been asked whether he was a poet or a surgeon, he would have unequivocally said poet. Just my opinion. A posthumous thanks to him as well.

Anyway, I've been very lucky to have all of these people in my life to support and encourage me, and, in many cases, for being good sports. I may not be a world-traveler, but between my (may I say crazy?) family, and my multi-faceted friends, I need only to travel to the little desk my dad made for my daughter. It is where I think, twist facts, and laugh myself silly. This little desk is surrounded by pictures, quotes, prayer flags, and ephemera. It is my sanctuary.

This book was finalized during a very strange time in our history—just when we thought it couldn't get any stranger. We are wearing designer masks to match our clothes and refraining from hugs. We are shopping online obsessively—our carts are full, credit cards maxed. We're trying to pay bills, we're mourning the death of over one hundred and eighty thousand people (at last count), from an insidious virus called COVID-19. We are living our lives in a far more isolated fashion, which brings about collateral damage like depression, over-indulging in a multitude of ways, and a general failure to thrive.

There is a maniac in the White House, and racial unrest in a century when there should no longer be issues of racial injustice, systemic or otherwise.

But on the bright side (if we can find one), we have become more creative—more politically involved. We are finding ways to gather safely. We're getting in touch with people we haven't thought about during our busy, previous existences. We are making it a point to tell the people in our lives how much they are loved and appreciated.

The sun continues to come up every morning, even if it can't be seen through the apocalyptic smoke from thousands of fires up and down the west coast. It is still there.

I hope these stories make you smile and take you out of whatever it is you might be dealing with, if only for a moment.

The story "Repetition Repeats Itself" is dedicated to the memory of Joan Taylor, who passed away April sixteenth, two thousand twenty.

If you would like to see a sweet, little film that my friend Janet Lee made from one of my stories, which is not included in this book, you can find it at https://youtu.be/MwaiKKoRR8M.

If you like the book, it would be great to know. I would also like your thoughts on a book of poetry. Would poetry interest you? Contact me at Lestercat16@gmail.com.

I wish everyone a fluffy-down-comforter-scented-with-lavender landing at the bottom of your daily ventures into your personal laundry chutes.

Xoxoxoxoxoxoxox

About the Author

Deborah Cashon Klein, D. Klein, resides in Safety Harbor, Florida. She likens herself to a yo-yo that has traveled from Ohio down to Florida, then up to Ohio, then down to Florida until there was no momentum left to go back up again.

She began writing at the age of seven in her hometown of Canfield, Ohio. Her dad found an old Radio Flyer wagon, which she used to sell her literary gems door-to-door. She composed fortunes on strips of paper that she rolled and inserted into drug capsules found in the garage. She also wrote greeting cards and little story books with hand-written pages stapled together. Her neighbors were good sports.

She has contributed essays and stories to a number of papers and journals in the Tampa Bay area, such as the *St. Pete Times Sunday Journal*, *Sunrise* (a small paper in Dunedin that people used for lining their birdcages), and *Tropical Breeze*, a really cool paper in Safety Harbor before newsprint became extinct, where she was a featured columnist. More recently, she was a literary editor for the *Huff/Post 50 Fiction Series* and has served as an editor and contributor to *Odet*, a Florida-centric literary journal. She is also an accomplished poet, and was recognized as *Creative Loafing's* Best Local Poet for the Tampa Bay metro area in 2015.

She has a daughter, Kristin, who lives in San Francisco.

CPSIA information can be obtained
at www.ICGtesting.com
Printed in the USA
BVHW031801060121
597088BV00003B/213